BIG
IDEAS
OF SCIENCE
REFERENCE LIBRARY

DK

BIG
IDEAS
OF SCIENCE
REFERENCE LIBRARY

PEARSON

Boston, Massachusetts
Chandler, Arizona
Glenview, Illinois
Upper Saddle River, New Jersey

ISBN-13: 978-0-13-369870-1
ISBN-10: 0-13-369870-X

1 2 3 4 5 6 7 8 9 10   V057   14 13 12 11 10

CONTENTS

KEY
These symbols appear in the top right corner below the topic name to connect the topic to the branches of science.

Earth Science   Life Science   Physical Science

BIG IDEAS OF EARTH SCIENCE 🌎

The Big Ideas of earth science help us understand our changing planet, its long history, and its place in the universe. Earth scientists study Earth and the forces that change its surface and interior.

Earth is part of a system of objects that orbit the sun.

Asteroids
Astronomy Myths
Bay of Fundy
Comets
Constellations
Earth
Gravity
Jupiter's Moons
Mars
Mars Rover
Mercury
Meteorites
Moon
Neptune
Pluto
Saturn
Solar Eclipse
Solar Power
Space Probes
Summer Solstice
Uranus
Venus

Earth is 4.6 billion years old and the rock record contains its history.

Atmosphere
Dating Rocks
Deep Sea Vents
Dinosaurs
Eryops
Extinction
Family Tree
Fossils
Geologic Time
Giant Mammals
Ice Age

Earth's land, water, air, and life form a system.

Altitude
Atacama Desert
Atmosphere
Aurora Borealis
Buoys
Doppler Radar
Dust Storms
Earth's Core
Floods
Fog
Gliding
Predicting Hurricanes
Rainbows
Sailing
Snowmaking
Storm Chasing
Thunderstorms
Weather Fronts

Earth is the water planet.

Amazon River
Beaches
Drinking Water
Everglades
Great Lakes
Mid-Ocean Ridge
Niagara Falls
Ocean Currents
Sea Stacks
Surfing
Thermal Imaging
Tsunami
Upwelling
Water

Earth is a continually changing planet.

Acid Rain
Afar Triangle
Caves
Coal

Colorado Plateau
Colorado River
Coral Reefs
Crystals
Dunes
Earthquakes
Equator
Fluorescent Minerals
Geocaching
Geodes
Geysers
Glaciers
Gold Mining
Hoodoos
Ice Age
Islands
Kilauea
Landslides
Lava
Mapping
Marble Quarries
Mid-Ocean Ridge
Mount Everest
Niagara Falls
Rain Forest
Rubies
Sea Stacks
Soil
Terrace Farming
Tour de France
Tsunami

Human activities can change Earth's land, water, air, and life.

Air Pollution
Energy Conservation
Equator
Fuel Cell Cars
Global Warming
Ice Age
Ocean Currents
Rain Forest
Shelter

The universe is very old, very large, and constantly changing.

Big Bang Theory
Black Holes
Constellations
Hubble Space Telescope
Milky Way
Quasars
Universe

Science, technology, and society affect each other.

Astronauts
Hubble Space Telescope
Jetpacks
International Space
  Station
Mars Rover
Predicting Hurricanes
Robots
Satellite Dish
Science at Work
Space Technology
Space Tourism
Virtual World

Scientists use mathematics in many ways.

Buoys
Doppler Radar
Mars Rover
Measurement
Neptune

Scientists use scientific inquiry to explain the natural world.

Extinction
Predicting Hurricanes
Wind Power
Neptune

BIG IDEAS OF LIFE SCIENCE 🐸

Life scientists study organisms, their life processes, and how they interact with one another and their environment. The Big Ideas of life science help us understand how living things are organized, how they get and use energy, and how they reproduce.

Living things grow, change, and reproduce during their lifetimes.

Animal Communication
Bush Baby
Courtship Rituals
Echolocation
Gorillas
Hummingbirds
Hypothalamus
Instinct
Marsupials
Menstrual Cycle
Penguins
Pregnancy
Puberty
Sea Horse
Seals
Sleep
Sloth
Tasmanian Devil
Twins
Worms

Living things are made of cells.

Blood Types
Cactus
Cell Division
Microscopes
Quarks and Leptons
Scent Pollution
Skeletons

Living things are alike yet different.

Adaptations
Aerogels
Bacteria
Bats
Bears
Cactus
Common Cold
DNA Connections
Exoskeleton
Family Tree
Farming
Ferns
Flowers
Frankenfoods
Fungi
Geckos
Giant Mammals
Gila Monster
Insects
Jellyfish
Naming
Patterns in Nature
Plant Tricks
Rain Forest
Red Tide
Redwoods
Scent Pollution
Skeletons
Snakes
Soil
Spiders
Survival
Symmetry
Taco Science
Whales

Living things interact with their environment.

Acid Rain
Air Pollution
Amazon River
Atacama Desert
Bats
Bay of Fundy
Beaches
Biodiversity
Biofuels
Bush Baby
Butterflies
Camouflage
Coal
Colorado Plateau
Deep Sea Vents
Energy Conservation
Everglades
Farming
Forestry
Frozen Zoo
Fuel Cell Cars
Georges Bank

Global Warming
GPS Tracking
Great Lakes
Hybrid Vehicles
Insects
Islands
Kilauea
Light Bulbs
Mid-Ocean Ridge
Mount Everest
Oil Spills
Patterns in Nature
Plant Invasion
Plastic
Population Growth
Rain Forest
Recycling
Red Tide
Renewal
Sea Horse
Seaweed
Seed Bank
Sharks
Shelter
Skywalk

Sloth
Soil
Solar Power
Supercooling Frogs
Sushi
Upwelling
Vultures

Genetic information passes from parents to offspring.

Blood Types
Colorblindness
DNA Evidence
Frankenfoods
Frozen Zoo
Genetic Disorders
Human Genome Project
Hummingbirds
Mutations
Probability

Living things get and use energy.

Algae
Barracuda
Birds
Cell Division
Elephants
Hummingbirds
New Body Parts
Octopus
Scorpion
Sea Horse
Seals
Sour Milk
Tasmanian Devil
Teeth

Structures in living things are related to their functions.

ACL Tear
Aerobic Exercise
ALS
Altitude
Animal Bodies
Birds
Blood Pressure
Blood Types
Brain Power
Broken Bones
Defibrillators
Digestion
Dolphins
Drinking Water
Exoskeleton
Fats

Gliding
Hearing Loss
Heartbeat
Hummingbirds
Jellyfish
Kidney Transplant
Laser Eye Surgery
Left vs. Right Brain
Marsupials
No Smoking
Open-Heart Surgery
Prosthetic Limb
Scent Pollution
Sea Turtles
Simulators
Singing
Skeletons
Skin
Sleep
Sloth
Steroids
Superfoods
Teeth
The Bends
Tour de France
Tweeters and Woofers
Vitamins and Minerals
Weightlifting

Living things change over time.

DNA Connections
Family Tree
Gorillas
Islands
Madagascar
Racehorses

Living things maintain constant conditions inside their bodies.

Allergies
Astronauts
Cancer Treatment
Common Cold
HIV/AIDS
Malaria
Marathon Training
Mold
MRI
Pandemic
Rats
Rheumatoid Arthritis
Scent Pollution
Sleep
Thermal Imaging
Vaccines
Working Body

Scientists use mathematics in many ways.

Census
Estimation
Hazardous Materials
Measurement
Probability
Simulators

Science, technology, and society affect each other.

Biomimetics
Clinical Trials
DNA Evidence
Eye Scan
Human Genome Project
Prosthetic Limb
Robots
Science at Work
Truth in Advertising

Scientists use scientific inquiry to explain the natural world.

BPA
Crittercam
Forensics
Human Genome Project
Naming
Quarks and Leptons
Truth in Advertising

BIG IDEAS OF PHYSICAL SCIENCE ⊛

Physical scientists study matter and energy. The Big Ideas of physical science help us describe the objects we see around us and understand their properties, motions, and interactions.

A net force causes an object's motion to change.

Asteroids
Astronauts
Bridges
Collision
Crew
Drag Racing
Formula 1 Car
Gravitron
Gravity
Hockey
Hovercraft
Jetpacks
Meteorites
Quasars
Roller Coaster
Sailing
Skydiving
Snowboard
Tour de France

Energy can take different forms but is always conserved.

Aerogels
ALS
Aurora Borealis
Bicycles
Black Holes
Bridges
Bungee Jumping
Catapults
Cordless Drill
Crew
Defibrillators
Earth's Core
Energy Conservation
Geocaching
Gliding
Headphones
Hoover Dam
Hybrid Vehicles
Lichtenberg Figures
Lifting Electromagnets
Light Bulbs
Microscopes
MP3 Player
MRI
Niagara Falls
Radio
Roller Coaster
Rube Goldberg Devices
Skyscraper
Skywalk
Submarines
Taco Science
Thermal Imaging
Weightlifting

Waves transmit energy.

Animal Communication
Cellphone
Color
Digital Camera
Doppler Radar
Echolocation
Eye Scan
Fluorescent Minerals
Geocaching
GPS Tracking
Guitar
Headphones
Hearing Loss
Holograms
Hubble Space Telescope
Hummingbirds
Laser Eye Surgery
Lighthouse
Microscopes
Mirages
Night Vision Goggles
Predicting Hurricanes
Radio
Rainbows
Rubies
Satellite Dish
Sea Stacks
Seaweed
Singing
Solar Power
Sonic Booms
Surfing
Thunderstorms
Tsunami
Tweeters and Woofers
Virtual World

Atoms are the building blocks of matter.

Acid Rain
Black Holes
Body Protection
Caves
Creating Elements
Crystals
Geckos
Glass

Gold Mining
Mars Rover
Melting Point
Meteorites
Nuclear Medicine
Prosthetic Limb
Quarks and Leptons
Steel
The Bends
Water

Mass and energy are conserved during physical and chemical changes.

Digestion
Earth
Fire Extinguishers
Fireworks
Forestry
Hovercraft
Ice Houses
Lava
Melting Point
Scent Pollution
Snowmaking
Supercooling
Frogs
The Bends

Scientists use mathematics in many ways.

Buoys
Hazardous Materials
Mars Rover
Measurement
Wind Tunnel

Scientists use scientific inquiry to explain the natural world.

Biomimetics
Forensics
Quarks and Leptons
Wind Power

Science, technology, and society affect each other.

Bridges
Cellphone
Formula 1 Car
Hubble Space
  Telescope
Light Bulbs
Prosthetic Limb
Robots
Science at Work

FATS

The human body has a love-hate relationship with fat. Our bodies have many uses for fats: They produce energy, process vitamins, and keep us warm. Fats are a key part of our cells and brains. But they can also be dangerous. Adults, adolescents, and children should get no more than 20 to 35 percent of their daily calories from fat. Many Americans approach 40 percent fat in their diets. Too much fat can cause obesity and lead to other health problems. Infants need more fat than adults, because fats are building blocks for brain development. There are two basic types of fats, saturated and unsaturated. Saturated fats, such as those found in meat, cheese, and other animal products, should be eaten in moderation. Unsaturated fats, such as those found in nuts and oils, are beneficial.

WHAT'S THE DIFFERENCE?

Different types of fat have different components. Fat molecules are long chains of carbon atoms with hydrogen atoms attached. If all the spaces around a carbon atom are filled with hydrogen atoms, the fat is called *saturated*. If there are empty spaces around a carbon atom, the fat is called *unsaturated*. There are two kinds of unsaturated fats: monounsaturated, with one empty space; and polyunsaturated, with more than one.

The green oil in the bottle is pressed from avocados, a monounsaturated fat like olive oil. It is a good source of vitamin E, which has been shown to protect against heart disease.

Pumpkin oil, a polyunsaturated fat, comes from pumpkin seeds. The oil can be almost black, like the one shown in the bottle to the right of the seeds. Pumpkin seeds have been shown to improve bone health.

Sesame oil is a polyunsaturated fat. Sesame seeds, which can produce an amber or lighter color oil, have been grown for thousands of years.

Most of the fat in butter is saturated. Many people substitute olive oil for butter when they cook so that they eat less saturated fat.

Olive oils contain monounsaturated fats. Virgin or extra virgin olive oils have the highest levels of nutrients, and are darker and more green than the light yellow oil shown here.

Walnuts have a polyunsaturated fat, omega-3 fatty acids, which are essential to healthy brains and hearts. Their oil is light in color and expensive.

A special kind of polyunsaturated fat called *omega-3 fatty acids,* found in fish such as salmon and tuna, is thought to reduce the risk of heart disease.

The white streaks in steak are lines of fat, called marbling. Fat in meat is mostly saturated and should be eaten in moderation.

Hazelnuts, or filberts, are about 55 percent fat. Most of this fat is monounsaturated and has a strong, nutty flavor..

Natural lard, which is melted pig fat, is mostly monounsaturated fat. However, most solid lard sold in supermarkets has had hydrogen atoms added to make it last longer. Unfortunately this also changes it into an unhealthy fat.

did you know? SIXTY PERCENT OF YOUR BRAIN IS MADE OF FAT.

If a fat is liquid at room temperature, it is typically healthy. Most of these fats are plant-based oils.

◄ THE GOOD, THE BAD, AND THE FATTY

There are two kinds of unhealthy fats: saturated fats and trans fats. These fats can clog arteries and increase the risk of heart disease and some cancers. Trans fats are called *hydrogenated*, because they are created by adding hydrogen atoms to existing fats. These are the worst fats to eat. They're very common, though, because hydrogenating fat gives it a longer shelf life. Trans fats are found in fried foods, prepared snacks such as cookies and crackers, and margarines, among others. Much healthier are polyunsaturated fats, which are liquid at room temperature, and monounsaturated fats, which remain liquid even in the refrigerator. Good fats can reduce the risk of some serious illnesses, especially if they replace bad fats in the diet.

Sunflower oil, pressed from sunflower seeds, is high in polyunsaturated fats, but is best used raw, because heating can produce harmful substances.

FERNS

In the world of plants, ferns may appear to be fragile and delicate, but their looks are deceiving. Although most ferns are found in warm, tropical areas, ferns are hardy, widespread, and adaptable plants. They are found all over the world and can grow in forests, on the surface of ponds, and even in rocks. Ferns are the largest group of seedless, vascular (veined) plants on Earth. There are at least 11,000 known fern species and probably hundreds more that have yet to be discovered. Unlike flowering plants, ferns do not use seeds to reproduce. Instead, they release tiny structures called *spores* that are scattered by the wind. These spores develop into heart-shaped plants called *prothallia*, which are so small they are hard to notice in the wild. Sperm and eggs are produced on the prothallia. They combine to form embryos that grow out of the prothallia into new ferns.

From fern fossils we know that ferns belong to an ancient group of plants that evolved between 385 and 359 million years ago.

TREE FERNS ▶
Super-sized ferns are common in the world's tropical forests. They are called tree ferns and, even though they are not true trees, they can grow to be 80 feet (about 24 m) tall. Tree ferns don't have bark. Instead, their trunks are made of vertically growing rhizomes, or stems, covered by a sheath of durable roots.

FIDDLEHEADS ▼
Fern buds and leaves develop in a tightly coiled structure that looks like, and is called, a *fiddlehead*. As the young fern leaves mature, the fiddleheads begin to slowly unfurl. Fiddleheads are one of the most recognizable of a fern's features, although not all ferns have them. Some people consider fiddleheads a delicacy and collect, cook, and eat them each spring.

▲ THE COMMON WOODLAND FERN
One unpopular but common fern species is a woodland fern called *bracken*. It is found in temperate and tropical climates worldwide. Bracken is one of the first plants to colonize open ground, invading fields and pastureland.

A structure called an *indusium* protects clusters of the spore-producing structures called *sporangia*. Sporangia are found on the undersides of fern fronds.

The leaves of tree ferns can be up to 13 feet (almost 4 m) long.

did you
know?...............
NATIVE AMERICANS USED TO
SNACK ON THE SWEET TASTING
LICORICE FERN. THEY USED THE
LADY FERN TO MAKE TEA.

FIRE EXTINGUISHERS

One of the most essential tools in the kitchen or workshop is something you hope you will never have to use—a fire extinguisher. A fire extinguisher can help put out a small fire. To extinguish a fire, you need to know how fire works. In most cases, a source of heat causes oxygen from the air to combine with a fuel—such as wood, cooking oil, or gasoline. These chemical reactions produce water and carbon dioxide, among other chemicals. Of course, fire produces a vast amount of energy in the form of heat and light—a flame. The heat produced by the fire provides the energy needed to burn even more fuel. In this way, a fire can quickly get out of hand. A fire will burn until it uses up the fuel or the oxygen—or until someone puts it out by interrupting the chemical reaction. Fire extinguishers do this by smothering or cooling the fire, or by insulating or removing the fuel.

Hard protective helmet

Heavy insulated jacket

▼ PULL OR TAP

Most types of fire extinguishers are easy to operate: just pull the pin and squeeze! PASS is an abbreviation for the actions you need to take. **P**ull the pin. **A**im the nozzle. **S**queeze the handle. **S**weep the spray at the the base of the flame. To activate some foam fire extinguishers, you must bump them while holding them upside down. This action opens a small container of acid inside the extinguisher. When acid mixes with a surrounding solution of base, such as bicarbonate of soda, carbon dioxide is produced. The pressurized gas mixes with the liquid, producing foam that shoots out of the extinguisher's nozzle.

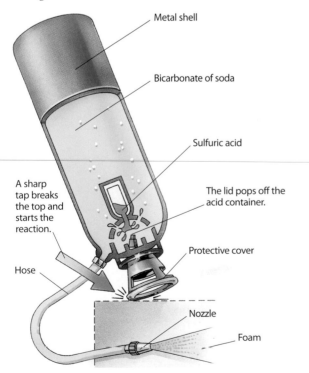

Metal shell

Bicarbonate of soda

Sulfuric acid

A sharp tap breaks the top and starts the reaction.

The lid pops off the acid container.

Protective cover

Hose

Nozzle

Foam

CHOOSING THE RIGHT EXTINGUISHER ▶

When there is a fire, the most important thing to do is call the fire department before the fire spreads. If you do use a fire extinguisher, you need to use the right one. Fire types are classified as A, B, C, or D, and the appropriate fire extinguisher to use on a fire is labeled with these same letters. Class A fires burn regular combustible material, such as paper or wood. Class B fires are fueled by liquid, such as gasoline or grease. Class C fires are caused by electrical equipment. Class D fires involve specific metals.

A water extinguisher can put out a Class A—wood or paper—fire, but it can cause a grease fire to spread. It can electrocute you during an electrical fire.

A foam extinguisher coats the fuel with a layer of foam that both insulates the fuel from heat and smothers the fire. It is used for flammable liquid (Class B) and electrical (Class C) fires. It can also be used on a Class A fire.

Carbon dioxide is heavier than oxygen. When you use a carbon dioxide extinguisher, the heavier gas pushes the oxygen out of the way. It also cools as it expands, which cools the fire. It is effective on liquid and electrical fires.

Dry chemical extinguishers spray a fine powder that does not burn as hotly as the fuel. The powder coats the fuel and smothers the fire. Most dry chemical extinguishers can work on any fire, but for Class A fires, water should be used as well.

**did you
know?**............................
FIRE PRODUCES ODORLESS, COLORLESS FUMES THAT CAN MAKE YOU SLEEPY, BUT THEY WILL SET OFF A SMOKE DETECTOR.

FIREWORKS

If fireworks sound like gunshots to you, it might be because they rely on the same chemical reaction—the burning of black powder. Black powder is another name for gunpowder. It is a mixture of sulfur, charcoal (primarily carbon), and saltpeter (a chemical that contains potassium, nitrogen, and oxygen). When lit, these chemicals react explosively, leading to a big bang, a bright light, lots of heat, and sometimes, injuries. The explosiveness of black powder compared with that of regular charcoal has to do with the way charcoal burns under different conditions. When charcoal is burned alone, it reacts slowly with the small supply of oxygen in the air around it. However, when mixed with the other ingredients of black powder, charcoal can react much more quickly with the oxygen in the saltpeter. The result is a fast reaction that can be used to create the exciting (and loud) displays of a fireworks show.

◄ FIRECRACKERS

Firecrackers are simply small packages of black powder that make a big bang when lit. Some come as a string of firecrackers, having short fuses that are attached to a long fuse. This arrangement lets people light only the long fuse to set off several firecrackers in a row. Firecrackers are illegal in some states.

Fuse

◄ LAUNCHING AN AERIAL

Display fireworks come in aerial shells. A worker places a shell in a launching pipe called a *mortar* and lights a fuse. This fuse, inside the pipe, ignites a small amount of black powder, called the *lift charge*. The burning of the lift charge launches the shell into the air and ignites a time-delayed fuse that keeps the shell from exploding until it reaches a safe height above the crowd. This second fuse ignites the bursting charge.

The bursting charge causes the shell to explode.

The explosion ignites the surrounding black powder and sends it out in all directions.

Throughout the black powder are objects called *stars*. These balls of fuel, burn to give fireworks their different colors.

FIREWORKS OVER THE BROOKLYN BRIDGE ►

Fireworks designers use different materials and packing arrangements to design the different colors, shapes, and timing effects of fireworks. Smaller stars burn more quickly than larger stars. Stars that contain strontium burn red. Those with barium burn green. Sodium makes a yellow light, while titanium makes a silver light. By building stars with different layers of materials that burn at different times, fireworks designers can create dramatic color changes.

did you know?............
FIREWORKS BURN AT TEMPERATURES GREATER THAN 3,600°F (2,000°C). THIS TEMPERATURE IS NEARLY TWICE AS HOT AS A CHARCOAL FIRE.

FLOODS

Although water is necessary for all life, a flood is too much of a good thing. Floods most often occur because more rain falls than an area can absorb in a given period of time. This can cause landslides, broken dams, and rising rivers. When rivers rise slowly, people may have time to leave the area before water overflows the banks. When torrential rain quickly sweeps into an area, it can cause what is called a *flash flood*. Because these floods happen too quickly for people to get to higher ground, flash floods can cause many deaths. Tsunamis, hurricanes, and broken dams can create dangerous waves, storm surges, or moving walls of water that overrun everything in their path. Entire drainage systems can overflow, especially in urban areas where there is not enough open land to soak up the water. Over the last century, the highest death toll—several million people—from a natural disaster was from a 1931 flood in China.

SOUTHERN CHINA, 2008 ▼
In June of 2008, large areas of southern China experienced day after day of heavy rainfall. Because the water level rose slowly, many people were able to evacuate. The floods caused landslides; destroyed homes, roads, and crops; and displaced more than a million people.

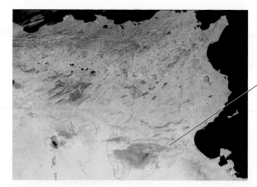

Depressions in the land, called *salt pans*, collect water, until the water evaporates.

On January 4, 2003, Tunisia is at the start of the winter rainy season.

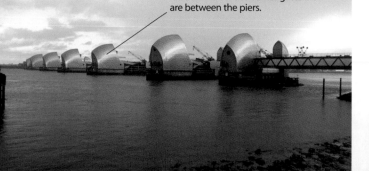

Giant piers contain the machines that raise and lower the barrier gates that are between the piers.

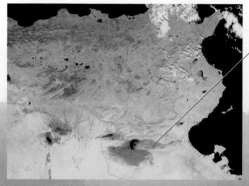

The darkening and spreading of the blue colors show that the water is deeper and that the salt-pan lakes have grown.

On January 19, 2003, more areas of blue and gray show flooding.

◀ NORTHERN AFRICA, 2003

Extreme conditions—cold temperatures, very heavy rains, and snow in mountainous areas—caused floods in northern Tunisia and Algeria during the winter of 2003. NASA photographs taken about two weeks apart show more snow and water, in shades of blue. Flooding drove 3,000 people from their homes.

▲ THE THAMES BARRIER

The Thames Barrier is the largest movable flood barrier in the world. It protects the city of London from flooding. Normally, the barrier gates are lowered to allow the Thames River to flow and ship traffic to pass. During tidal surges, the barrier gates are raised to hold back water that travels up the river from the sea.

A survivor guides his craft atop water-clogged streets to get his passenger to safety.

did you know?
SOME ENGINEERS PROPOSE A "GIVE WATER SPACE" POLICY FOR THE NETHERLANDS AND NEW ORLEANS: A PLAN TO BUILD CANALS AND STORAGE AREAS FOR WATER TO FLOW INTO, NOT JUST DIKES AND LEVEES TO KEEP WATER OUT.

FLOWERS

Flowers are loved all over the world for their sweet smells and beautiful colors, but sometimes they are deadly. Certain flowers are so poisonous that children have died from eating them or from drinking vase water. Other flowers are edible and nutritious. With over 400,000 species, flowers have a variety of sizes, shapes, colors, and smells. Some, such as the dandelion, are familiar because they grow in so many places. Others, such as the giant *Rafflesia,* are rare and have unusual characteristics. You might think of a flower as a plant with colorful blossoms, but to a scientist, a flower is only the reproductive part of a plant: the part that makes seeds. Strong smells and bright petals attract insects. The reward for visiting is a sugary liquid food called *nectar*. Pollen sticks to insects when they eat, and they transport the pollen between flowers. Parts of the pollen then fertilize eggs, which develop into seeds.

Fruit containing seed is carried into the air.

FLYING FRUIT ▶

Dandelion seeds have feathery parachutes to help them fly far from their parent plant. A dandelion is made up of many small flowers, called *florets*. Each floret develops a single fruit. The fruits form inside the closed-up seed head, after the yellow petals have withered away. When the weather is dry, the seed head opens, revealing a ball of parachutes. The slightest breeze lifts the parachutes into the air.

The parachute remains attached to the seed head until a gust of wind picks it up.

The flower head opens daily. Insects get nectar from the flower but do not pollinate it.

The open seed head reveals fully formed fruits, each attached to a tiny parachute.

Seeds develop inside the closed flower head.

did you know? HONEY BEES VISIT ABOUT TWO MILLION FLOWERS TO MAKE ONE POUND (0.5 KG) OF HONEY.

RAFFLESIA ▼

Not all flowers have the sweet smell you might expect. The world's largest flower is a species of *Rafflesia*. This enormous flower smells like rotting meat. The smell is repulsive to most people (although it doesn't seem to be bothering these kids), but it attracts insects that pollinate the flower. It has no stem, leaves, or roots. Instead, it lives as a parasite. It obtains nutrients from thin strands of tissue that extend into nearby vines. *Rafflesia* grows only in the rain forests of Southeast Asia.

❶ GIANT PETALS

A fully grown *Rafflesia* is about 3 feet (1 m) wide. The bud takes almost a year to mature. It then opens into 5 thick, fleshy petals which last only about a week before decomposing. This short time available for pollination is one reason the plant is rare.

❷ PROTECTIVE SPIKES

Hard spikes extend from the center region of the *Rafflesia*. In a female flower, these spikes protect thousands of eggs.

❸ RIM OF THE CUP

The rim of tissue around the central cup of a *Rafflesia* tends to keep the putrid smell close to the flower. The strong smell attracts more insects and increases the chance of pollination.

FLUORESCENT MINERALS

If you look closely at many different rocks, you will notice that some contain shiny crystals, or minerals. Minerals can form as molten rock cools, causing atoms to bond together. They can also form when water that contains dissolved elements evaporates, leaving the elements behind. Often the atoms of these elements are close enough to bond together to form crystals. A pure mineral is made up of a single compound and is usually colorless. Add a tiny amount of another element, or an impurity, and you can get some amazing effects. The brilliant green of an emerald and red of a ruby come from crystal impurities. Some minerals even seem to glow. Fluorescent minerals shine brightly when they are exposed to ultraviolet light, sometimes called *black light*. Many natural history museums have collections of these minerals. Under normal lighting, you see interesting shapes, often gray or brown in color. When the black light comes on, though, the room shines with bright yellows, reds, greens, and blues as the minerals give off these colors.

You often find several minerals together. Under the UV light, it is obvious that the quartz crystals surrounding the calcite are made of a different material.

▼ GLOWING IN THE DARK

Under normal lighting, this large calcite crystal appears as a white hexagonal column. This crystal contains an impurity—manganese ions. When the crystal is exposed to ultraviolet (UV) light, the electrons in the manganese absorb energy. Then they give off this energy in the form of reddish-orange light.

Fluorescence is a type of luminescence, light that is produced without heat. The energy comes from ultraviolet light.

GLOWING IN THE LIGHT ▲

The word *fluorescence* comes from the mineral fluorite, the first fluorescent mineral to be discovered. This blue color, caused by europium atoms in the crystal, is sometimes bright enough that the crystal glows in sunlight.

Different impurities produce different colors. Uranium in quartz produces green light, while mercury can produce pink or bright blue light.

did you know? THE FLUORESCENT MINERAL CAPITAL OF THE WORLD IS THE BOROUGH OF FRANKLIN IN NORTHERN NEW JERSEY.

FOG

We can see fog, but we can't touch it. So what is it? Fog is a cloud that forms close to the ground. Water is continuously evaporating from Earth's surface, adding water vapor to the air. Water vapor is water in a gaseous state, and it's invisible. Air can become what is called *saturated*—it holds as much water vapor as possible—also referred to as a condition of 100 percent humidity. As air cools, some of the water vapor condenses into liquid water droplets. As these water droplets form, they may cling to particles in the air, such as dust, pollution, or salt. A low-lying patch of water droplets clinging to particles is called *fog*. Such an area much higher in the atmosphere is called a *cloud*. Fog is defined as a condition in which visibility is less than 0.6 miles (about 1 km). When visibility is greater than 0.6 miles, the condition is called mist.

◄ FOG OVER MONT ST. MICHEL

France's Mont St. Michel is a rocky island surrounded by tidal mud flats. Fog forms here on clear nights when the mud cools. The cool mud also cools the air above it. The water droplets condense onto salt particles suspended in the air to create ground-level fog that rarely moves. It usually disappears after the sun rises, because warm air evaporates the water droplets.

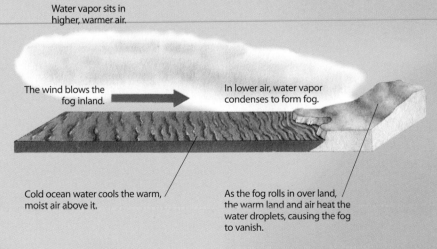

Water vapor sits in higher, warmer air.

The wind blows the fog inland.

In lower air, water vapor condenses to form fog.

Cold ocean water cools the warm, moist air above it.

As the fog rolls in over land, the warm land and air heat the water droplets, causing the fog to vanish.

◄ FOG ROLLS IN

Fog forms at sea when warm, moist air drifts over cold water. The water cools the air, and condensation takes place. Sea fog is "glued" together when condensed water attaches to salt particles tossed into the air by crashing waves. Salt is an unusual condensation particle. It will allow fog to form when the humidity is only 70 percent—that's less than complete saturation.

Wind currents created by the airplane's wing tips cut a swath in the fog, causing the edges to curl in a spiral shape called a *vortex*.

SMOG FORMS WHEN WATER VAPOR CONDENSES ON POLLUTION PARTICLES, OFTEN FROM CAR EXHAUST.

Air currents can push fog into unusual shapes or patterns. Here ridges are formed below as a plane passes through fog.

Flying through fog is risky without proper training. Student pilots must master flying in clear conditions before traveling through fog.

◄ FLYING IN FOG

Fog can create an optical illusion for pilots. They report feeling that the plane's nose is pointing up. Pilots unaware of this illusion will turn the nose down too quickly. Commercial airline pilots who fly planes through fog use the instrument panel for navigation. In the fog, a pilot cannot use vision or other senses to tell up from down, and must rely on technology to guide the plane.

FORENSICS

Television crime and police shows paint an exciting picture of the job of a forensic scientist, but discoveries may take weeks or months of research and analysis, as opposed to the hour it takes to get results on TV. Forensics requires the same skills necessary in all fields of science. Forensic scientists must gather evidence and analyze it, develop a hypothesis, and present their results in order to understand what happened at a crime scene. They can determine who was present when a person died by studying DNA samples, fibers taken from a scene, and the condition of the body. Proving how a victim died can be more difficult, though. For example, proving whether a person drowned or was dead before entering the water is not as simple as it appears on television. Water in the lungs does not prove that a person drowned, because water can enter the lungs of a dead person placed under water.

The FBI has developed a computerized system to match crime-scene prints to fingerprints on file.

Scientists use the ridges of fingerprints to help identify their owner. Often, only partial prints are available, making them difficult to match.

WATCH THEIR STEPS ▼

Shoe prints are a common type of evidence left at crime scenes. Each one is different, making shoe prints a valuable clue for forensic scientists. If a shoe is old, the tread may be worn. Marks and scratches that appear on some shoe prints can help with identification. But they aren't perfect. Unlike fingerprints, shoe soles change over time, making prints harder to link to a suspect. Scientists are working on improving shoe-print analysis.

Scientists can analyze a shoe print to tell what size, type, and, perhaps, even what brand of shoe a suspect wore!

FINDING FINGERPRINTS ▶

Whenever you touch something, you leave behind a fingerprint. Everyone's prints are unique. If scientists find a fingerprint at a crime scene, they can check it against an FBI database, which contains more than 250 million sets of prints. A fingerprint match can help prove a suspect was at a crime scene. Scientists use powder to show fingerprints on hard surfaces. They use chemicals to find prints on documents.

◀ BODY OF EVIDENCE

Organic samples taken from the human body contain valuable information. Scientists in crime labs collect and analyze these samples—blood, saliva, urine, stomach contents, and more. By analyzing these substances, scientists can draw conclusions about the cause of death. They can also tell a person's blood type and whether a blood sample is human.

MT97–55233

If a body is found, scientists can examine the stomach contents for signs of drugs, poisons, or medications.

Scientists who analyze urine samples have pointed out that it can be difficult to distinguish between evidence of illegal drugs made from poppies and foods that contain poppy seeds.

MT97–56301

A blood sample is packed with identifying information, including tiny bits of DNA and unusual proteins or enzymes.

did you know?

WILDLIFE FORENSIC SCIENTISTS EXAMINE EVIDENCE TO SEE IF IT CONTAINS ILLEGAL ANIMAL PRODUCTS, SUCH AS RHINOCEROS HORN, USED AS AN INGREDIENT IN SOME MEDICINES.

FORESTRY

If you could trace where your bedroom furniture, bicycle tires, or favorite chocolate bar originated, you'd probably find yourself in a tropical rain forest. Materials for clothing, fuel, and some medicines also come from rain forests. Temperate and tropical forests cover more than one fourth of Earth's land area. Large areas, however, are lost each year to deforestation. Deforestation occurs when people cut down forests to grow crops, raise cattle and sheep, harvest timber, and build cities. Deforestation destroys wildlife habitats. It can lead to soil erosion and global warming. Forestry—the science of managing forests and the wildlife, water, and resources in them—arose from the need to sustain, or maintain, forested areas so they don't completely disappear. Forestry practices such as managed tree harvesting and replanting help protect sources of fresh water and other resources.

GABON'S UNIQUE TREES ▼

Forests cover about 85 percent of Gabon, Africa. In 1913, loggers began harvesting *okoumé*, Gabon's most valuable wood, to make plywood. Between 1990 and 2000, Gabon lost about 25,000 acres of forest per year to logging. Today, more than 50 companies harvest in Gabon's forests, home to about 8,000 plant species—more than in all the rest of West African forests combined. New laws in Gabon encourage sustainable logging practices.

Gabon is the largest exporter of wood in West Africa. Loggers use chain saws to cut down the trees. Then they trim and skid (pull) the trees out of the forest

WHY GROW TREES? ▲

In 1941, loggers were cutting down forests at alarming rates without replanting. In response, scientists started the first tree farm in Washington State. Today, tree farms help regenerate forests that have been logged. Foresters plant seedlings in a logged-over area. The seedlings grow to mature trees. Reforesting and practicing conservation now will help insure that future generations have enough natural resources to meet their needs.

did you know?
ABOUT HALF OF THE FORESTS THAT ORIGINALLY COVERED EARTH'S SURFACE ARE GONE. DEMAND FOR TIMBER PRODUCTS IS ESTIMATED TO DOUBLE IN THE NEXT 25 YEARS.

This clawlike device is a hydraulic log grapple fork. It clamps onto a log and lifts it into place.

LOSING THE RAIN FORESTS ▼

NASA satellite photos document the rapid disappearance of the Bolivian rain forest. Loggers have cut roads through the forests, and farmers have cleared large areas for farms and ranches.

This satellite image above shows green forested areas near Santa Cruz, Bolivia, in 1984. Government subsidies encouraged the spread of soybean farms.

By 1996, the forest area cleared for farming had grown in size. The powerful soybean lobby was able to win government support for its farms. The grid pattern in the upper left shows government farms.

This wheel loader places logs onto the bed of a logging truck. The truck transports the logs to a sawmill.

FORMULA 1 CAR

At 200 miles per hour (about 322 km/h), a vehicle with wings could fly. Formula 1 cars reach that speed and do have wings attached to the front and back of the car. Their wings, however, are designed to create the opposite of lift, called *downforce*. This downward force allows cars to cling tightly to the track as they maneuver the tight curves of a Formula 1 race. However, this force also slows the car down. The other force slowing the car down is the force of the air pushing against the car as it moves forward. Every part of the car is designed to minimize these forces, by allowing air to move smoothly over, under, and around the car. The goal in designing these cars is to achieve the highest speed without flying off the track. This balance can get pretty tricky when 0.01 second can be the difference between winning and losing the race.

did you know?
FORMULA 1 CARS PRODUCE SO MUCH DOWNFORCE THAT, AT 100 MILES PER HOUR (ABOUT 161 KM/H), THEY COULD THEORETICALLY BE DRIVEN UPSIDE DOWN ON A CEILING.

WINDING ALONG THE TRACK ▼
In the first automobile race, held in France in 1894, the average speed of the winning car was about 11 miles per hour (almost 18 km/h). Now around 20 Formula 1 races are held each year in countries around the world. The average speeds vary with the particular track, but on the straight portions, a Formula 1 car moves at least 180 miles per hour (almost 290 km/h)—much higher in some races.

GOING WITH THE FLOW

Wings, sometimes called *spoilers*, on the front and back of a Formula 1 car, are one of the most important design features. Their purpose is to direct air that is blasting against the car as it gains speed. Airplane wings are designed to direct the air that hits the wing downward, lifting the plane up. The rear wing on a Formula 1 car directs the air upward, so the back of the car is pressed down.

The rear wing tilts upward, directing the air up. This creates a low-pressure area under the wing that acts almost as a vacuum, sucking the rear tires against the track.

The front wing hits the air first. Its shape determines how the air will flow along the whole car.

Vertical end plates on the front wing reduce drag over the front tires.

The shape of the car body is rounded and decreases in width so that air flows over it with the least resistance.

The tires of a Formula 1 car have to be very light but still be able to handle a downforce of about 9,960 Newtons on each tire. Because of friction, the tires get as hot as boiling water.

FOSSILS

Fossils are like Earth's history book. They can show what lived where and when, and who ate what—or whom. Fossils have been discovered in some very unlikely places. Saber-toothed cats, mammoths, ground sloths, and prehistoric American lion fossils have been found in the middle of the city of Los Angeles! These fossils came from the site of La Brea Tar Pits, the largest and most diverse collection of plants and animals from the Ice Age. Fossils of more than 2,000 individual saber-toothed cats have been recovered from this site. But these fossils are very young—only 10,000 to 40,000 years old. Some of the oldest known fossils, which are of bacteria, are nearly 3.5 billion years old.

The root of the tooth was embedded in the cartilage of the jaw.

Trilobites are named for their three lobes that run head to tail.

◄ TRILOBITE

Trilobites are extinct arthropods—animals like crabs and insects—that lived in ancient seas as long ago as 530 million years. These creatures, which ranged in length from under a centimeter to more than 2 feet (70 cm), had particularly hard exoskeletons. They molted, or shed their exoskeletons, leaving behind many fossils, which are still found today. The trilobites' soft tissues, such as their legs, decomposed. Scientists have pieced together information about the trilobites using what they know about today's arthropods.

SHARK TOOTH ▲

Sharks' tooth fossils are abundant. When a tooth breaks and falls out of a shark's mouth, a new sharp one replaces it. One shark can shed thousands of teeth during its lifetime. Their teeth fossilize easily, so where there were prehistoric sharks, there are lots of shark tooth fossils.

The skull and tusks of *Gomphotherium* were more than 6.5 feet long (2 m).

Tusk

did you know? ONLY SEVEN *T. REX* SKELETONS THAT ARE MORE THAN HALF COMPLETE HAVE BEEN FOUND.

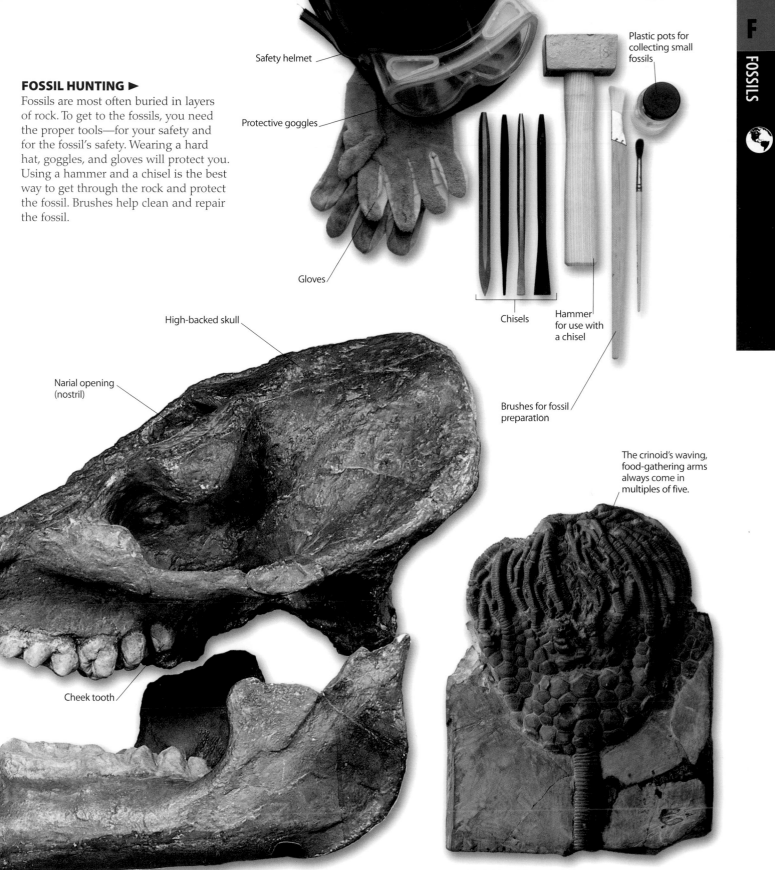

FOSSIL HUNTING ▶

Fossils are most often buried in layers of rock. To get to the fossils, you need the proper tools—for your safety and for the fossil's safety. Wearing a hard hat, goggles, and gloves will protect you. Using a hammer and a chisel is the best way to get through the rock and protect the fossil. Brushes help clean and repair the fossil.

Safety helmet

Protective goggles

Gloves

Plastic pots for collecting small fossils

Chisels

Hammer for use with a chisel

Brushes for fossil preparation

High-backed skull

Narial opening (nostril)

Cheek tooth

The crinoid's waving, food-gathering arms always come in multiples of five.

GOMPHOTHERIUM ▲

This skull from the *Gomphotherium* genus is about 20 million years old. *Gomphotheres* were ancestors of extinct mastodons and modern elephants. They had both upper and lower tusks, and most likely lived in lakes and swamps where they used their lower tusks to dig up the vegetation. *Gomphotherium* remains have been found in many parts of the world, including Germany, Kenya, and even in the middle of the United States, in Kansas.

FOSSIL CRINOID ▲

Although it looks like a plant, a crinoid is actually an animal called an *echinoderm*. It is a relative of sea urchins and sea stars. During the Paleozoic era, crinoids blanketed the sea floor. Experts have used their fossil records to identify hundreds of different species of crinoids, some of which still exist.

FRANKENFOODS

The fictional character, Victor Frankenstein, was obsessed with creating life. He used old body parts to build a creature. After he brought the creature to life, he was horrified by what he had made—a monster. Should people create new types of food crops, or is there a danger of creating "Frankenfoods"? Opponents of altering the genetic material of food crops use this nickname for genetically modified organisms, called *GMOs* or *transgenic* crops. They point out that GMOs may have unanticipated, harmful characteristics and effects. However, GMO supporters argue that transgenic crops can have positive characteristics, such as resistance to insects or higher vitamin content. Farmers long ago figured out how to selectively breed plants, called *hybrids*, that have the best characteristics of the parent plants. GMOs, on the other hand, are created by inserting the genetic material of one individual into that of another. There is a great deal of debate over the pros and cons of GMOs. Many questions remain about their safety for humans, their effect on unmodified crops, and the rules that will govern their use.

RICE ▼

Billions of people in Asia depend on rice as their main source of calories. Some rice now on the market has been genetically modified to contain more vitamin A (beta carotene), iron, and zinc. Vitamin A deficiency can cause malnutrition and blindness. One type of rice was developed using genes from daffodils and bacteria. Is it safe to eat this rice? In the short term, it appears that GMOs are safe. However, people have not been eating GMOs long enough for us to know whether there are any long-term effects.

did you know?......................
ABOUT 80 PERCENT OF THE CORN PLANTED IN THE UNITED STATES IN 2008 WAS FROM GENETICALLY MODIFIED SEED.

CORN ▼

Genes used to create GMOs may come from different types of organisms. For example, some insect-resistant corn has genetic material from a type of bacteria. Pollen from this corn has blown over the U.S. border or been planted by farmers in Mexico, where planting most GMO corn is banned. GMO opponents do not want this altered corn to breed with the native varieties of corn that grow in Mexico.

Although commercially grown strawberries are larger than these wild Alpine ones, they typically do not have their intense flavor.

The corn earworm is the most serious sweet-corn pest, feeding directly on corn kernels.

STRAWBERRIES ▲

Many opponents of GMO foods point out that plants can be bred to have certain traits over time, using traditional selective breeding techniques. Sometimes this happens naturally. Commercial strawberries that we eat today are a hybrid of two different strawberry plants that bred accidentally in Europe in the mid-1700s. These strawberries, larger than those of the parent plants, are now raised all over the world.

TOMATOES ▲

The first genetically modified tomatoes came onto the market in 1994. They were engineered so that they did not produce an enzyme that caused them to rot. This modification helped them stay fresh longer. However, they also contained genes that made them resistant to antibiotics. After doctors voiced concern that these genes could be transferred to bacteria in the human gut, these tomatoes were taken off the market.

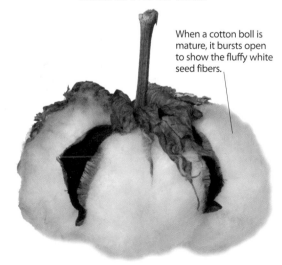

When a cotton boll is mature, it bursts open to show the fluffy white seed fibers.

◄ SOYBEANS

Nearly all soybeans produced in the United States come from genetically modified seeds. They are designed to be resistant to herbicides that are used to kill weeds. However, in 2009, more farmers began planting non-genetically modified soybeans again because the price of GMO seeds had become too high.

COTTON ▲

Cotton has been genetically modified to resist pests. The bollworm is an insect that can do extensive damage to cotton crops.

FROZEN ZOO

Polar bears, seals, Arctic foxes—perhaps you can imagine finding these animals at a zoo somewhere in the frozen Arctic Circle. A *frozen zoo*, however, is a very different kind of zoo. You won't find animals there—but you will find their sperm, eggs, embryos, blood, cell cultures, and tissues. Samples like these contain the animals' genetic material. An individual animal's genetic material, or DNA, is what determines the animal's size, shape, color, and other physical characteristics. Genetic material can also support an entire species' ability to survive. Scientists have been collecting and freezing the genetic material of endangered animals for more than 30 years. Why? Conservation. Genetic material helps scientists protect and strengthen endangered animal populations. With DNA, scientists can assist with breeding the animals to increase their number of offspring and improve an entire species' chances of avoiding extinction.

did you know?

IN 1980, ONLY 19 CALIFORNIA CONDORS REMAINED IN THE WILD. WITH CONSERVATION EFFORTS AND HELP FROM SAN DIEGO'S FROZEN ZOO, THERE ARE NOW MORE THAN 300 BIRDS, 135 OF THEM LIVING IN THE WILD.

SAN DIEGO'S FROZEN ZOO ▼

Samples of genetic material from more than 8,400 individual animals from 800 species and subspecies "live" at the Frozen Zoo at San Diego Zoo's Institute for Conservation Research. They include animals like the Gobi bear, secretary bird, and African clawed frog. Scientists at the Frozen Zoo track evolutionary trends and preserve genetic variation, or differences among individuals within a species. Species with diverse gene pools have a greater chance of survival.

You might see a Bengal tiger cub in a zoo. Only between 3,000 and 4,700 of these endangered cats remain in the wild.

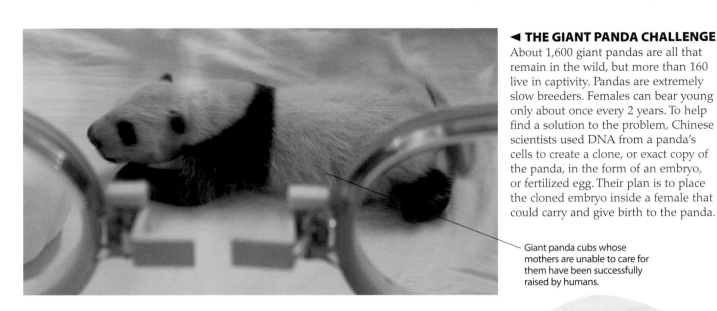

◄ THE GIANT PANDA CHALLENGE

About 1,600 giant pandas are all that remain in the wild, but more than 160 live in captivity. Pandas are extremely slow breeders. Females can bear young only about once every 2 years. To help find a solution to the problem, Chinese scientists used DNA from a panda's cells to create a clone, or exact copy of the panda, in the form of an embryo, or fertilized egg. Their plan is to place the cloned embryo inside a female that could carry and give birth to the panda.

Giant panda cubs whose mothers are unable to care for them have been successfully raised by humans.

◄ YELLOW SEA HORSE

The yellow sea horse population is declining. The species is used in traditional Chinese medicine and sold for use in aquariums. Its DNA, along with the DNA or tissue samples of about 1,000 species, has been preserved by the Frozen Ark Project at the University of Nottingham in England.

Ocean pollution and habitat destruction also contribute to the decreasing number of yellow sea horses.

CRYOSPRESERVATION

Frozen zoos use cryopreservation, the process of freezing and preserving genetic material. Scientists fill special holding tanks with liquid nitrogen that keeps the temperature of the samples at –320°F (–196°C). Frozen genetic material can be stored indefinitely, perhaps for thousands of years. If a species nears extinction, scientists can thaw the samples and use them to help animals produce young.

FUEL CELL CARS

Everyday, millions of people add carbon dioxide, nitrous oxide, and other greenhouse gases—gases that trap heat in the atmosphere—to the air, simply by driving to the grocery store. In fact, the largest source of carbon dioxide, the most common greenhouse gas, is transportation. Earth needs some greenhouse gases. Without them, the temperature of the planet would be much colder. But human activities, such as driving, have led to an increase in greenhouse gases, ultimately leading to global warming. The temperature of Earth's surface has increased about 1°F (about 0.56°C) in the last 100 years. If we could eliminate greenhouse gases from vehicle emissions and replace them with water vapor, the warming effect on Earth could be greatly reduced. Engineers and scientists have developed fuel cell cars that do just that. The fuel is hydrogen and oxygen, and the product is electricity, heat, and water!

Exhaust from fuel cell vehicles is clean. It contains no pollutants, only water vapor.

The fuel cell stack in the center of the vehicle combines hydrogen with oxygen, which generates electricity to power the vehicle.

Compressed hydrogen gas is stored in a high-pressure hydrogen tank.

did you know?

FUEL CELLS POWER THE ELECTRICAL SYSTEMS OF NASA'S SPACE SHUTTLES. THE CREW DRINKS THE WATER PRODUCED BY THE CELLS.

WHERE'S THE CLOSEST GAS STATION? ▶

Some obstacles to getting fuel cell cars on the road is the lack of pipelines, trucks, and storage facilities to deliver the hydrogen to the fueling stations. One company that makes hydrogen fuel cell cars, is developing a home energy station that can produce hydrogen from natural gas. It would provide heat and electricity for the home and fuel for fuel cell vehicles. Using a home energy station would make carbon dioxide emissions 30 percent lower overall than those of the average household.

◀ HYDROGEN FUEL CELL CAR

Hydrogen fuel cell cars are now available in places where hydrogen refueling stations exist. In Southern California, drivers can lease a car like the one shown here. The minivan shown above is being driven in Iceland, the location for some of the testing of hydrogen fuel cell vehicles.

HYDROGEN NOZZLE AND METER ▶

Filling up your car with hydrogen is slightly more complicated than filling it up with gasoline. Most fuel cell vehicles use gaseous hydrogen. The pump at the gas station has to read the pressure in the gas tank and determine how much fuel is needed. The nozzle is also different. It locks into place so that hydrogen cannot escape.

Nozzle

FUEL CELL HYBRID ▼

One company has created this fuel cell hybrid vehicle (FCHV), which is based on a popular SUV model. It is able to run either on electricity or fuel cells. The vehicle is being tested, but is not in production yet.

The electric drive motor of hydrogen fuel cell cars is exceedingly quiet, reducing noise pollution and making for a quiet, smooth ride.

FCHV
FUEL CELL HYBRID VEHICLE

FUNGI

Fungi are such unique organisms that they form their own scientific kingdom, whose members range from unicellular organisms such as yeast to multicellular organisms that can look similar to plants. But unlike plants, fungi don't have the chlorophyll needed to absorb sunlight and make nutrients. Instead, fungi secrete enzymes onto the surfaces where they grow, such as on wood, plants, fruit, or even dung. The enzymes cause the surface to decompose, and the fungi absorb the nutrients through a system of tiny threadlike cells, called the *mycelium*. When we see fungi, like the head and stem of a mushroom, or mold growing on bread, what we see is usually what's called the *fruiting body*. Often more than 90 percent of the fungus is composed of the underground mycelium. Fungi can live almost anywhere, including on plants and animals. Many plants have a symbiotic relationship with fungi. The plant gives the fungus some energy through photosynthesis. In return, the fungus helps the plant take up water and minerals.

TURKEY TAILS ▶

These leathery bracket fungi—shelflike growths—do resemble their name. They grow by breaking down dead wood. The result of this process is that nutrients from the tree return to the soil.

FLY AGARIC—BEWARE! ▼

Fly agaric is definitely not for eating! This fungus has been used to kill flies by attracting them to milk that has small pieces of the poisonous fungus soaking in it. The individual threadlike cells of fly agaric's mycelium, called *hyphae*, tap into tree roots to obtain nutrients.

The scarlet wax cap mushroom is brightly colored and feels waxy.

The mushroom's stem is called a *stape*.

Gills, where millions of reproductive structures called *spores* are produced

POWDER-FILLED PUFFBALLS ▶

The fruiting body of a puffball can be as tiny as a large pea or bigger than a watermelon. Calculations have shown that a soccer-ball sized giant puffball contains about 7 trillion spores. The largest giant puffball on record weighed in at a mighty 48 pounds (almost 22 kg) and was more than 8 feet (more than 2.6 m) in diameter!

know?..............
FOX FIRE—A LUMINESCENCE
THAT COMES FROM ROTTING
WOOD—IS CAUSED BY FUNGI
THAT GLOW IN THE DARK!

In large quantities, puffball spores appear as a fine powder. Individual spores are microscopic.

Poof! Clouds of microscopic spores escape from a split in the top of the puffball when conditions are right for dispersal.

The round or pear-shaped fruiting body of a mature puffball contains its spore dust, for reproduction.

Some puffballs have stems, but other varieties sit on top of rotting wood or directly on the ground.

The spore-filled puffball is the only visible part of the fungus. The hidden underground mycelium network is much larger.

GECKOS

Geckos are remarkable lizards that can climb walls and scamper upside down across ceilings. They can scale glass surfaces with ease, and they can even hang from a branch by a single toe! How do geckos accomplish these amazing climbing feats? Geckos have thousands of tiny hairs on each of their toes. These hairs are so tiny that the atoms in each hair attach to atoms on the surface the geckos walk on. The atoms in each hair are held in place by the same attractive forces that hold the particles in liquids and solids together. When enough hairs attach at the same time, they can support the weight of the entire gecko. Today scientists are trying to replicate gecko adhesion. If they are successful, one day you might hang pictures on walls without using nails or glue. Or you might be able to walk on ice without slipping.

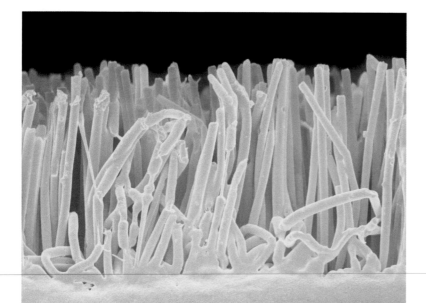

HAIRY FEET ▼

Geckos have ridges on their toes. Each ridge has thousands of tiny hairs. Each hair splits into many smaller hairs. In all, geckos may have a billion hairs touching the surface when they walk! Because each hair attaches weakly to surfaces, geckos can pull their feet off easily whenever they want.

CARBON NANOTUBES ▲

Nanotechnology is a new area of science in which researchers make extremely small materials. Something that measures at the high end of the nanoscale would be one thousand times smaller than the thickness of a sheet of paper. Scientists can make carbon nanotubes that resemble gecko hairs. These strong, tiny tubes stick 10 times better than the hairs on a gecko's foot.

Geckos have five toes on each foot. Hairs on each toe stick when the gecko drags its foot.

did you know? GECKO FEET FEEL SMOOTH AND SOFT AND ARE NOT AT ALL STICKY.

Most of the almost 1,000 species of gecko are 1.2 to 6 inches long (about 3–15 cm). The tokay gecko can grow to 14 inches long (almost 36 cm).

A gecko can attach and detach its feet from a surface 15 to 30 times per second! Geckos detach their toes from a surface by bending the toes backwards!

◄ MADAGASCAN DAY GECKO

The Madagascan day gecko, which can be almost a foot long (30 cm), runs up and down tree trunks, palm leaves, and house walls to catch insects and spiders. It does not have eyelids. Instead, clear membranes cover its eyes, which have round pupils. Geckos lay hard-shelled eggs. They need lots of calcium to make the egg shells, so female geckos store calcium in sacks on the sides of their heads.

If one foot loses its grip when a gecko climbs a slippery wall, the gecko taps its tail to the wall to balance.

A gecko's toe hairs are angled. They grip the surface when dragged in one direction and detach when dragged in the opposite direction.

If a predator attacks a gecko's tail, the gecko can escape because its tail will break off. It can regrow a shorter one.

The end of each of these gecko foot hairs, called *setae*, splits into as many as 1,000 even smaller hairs, called *spatulae*.

GENETIC DISORDERS

You have probably "caught" a cold, but you cannot "catch" a genetic disorder. A genetic disorder is a medical condition caused by a mutation—a permanent change—in someone's DNA (deoxyribonucleic acid), or by a change in the structure or number of a person's chromosomes. Your DNA is the set of instructions contained in almost every cell of your body. You inherit 23 chromosomes—bundles of DNA—from each parent. Together those chromosomes contain more than 20,000 genes. People with genetic disorders may have inherited an abnormal gene from one or both parents. Down syndrome, for example, is a genetic disorder that causes learning difficulties. It is caused by an extra chromosome inherited from one parent. Other genetic disorders may be caused by a gene that becomes damaged or lost during development. Either way, there is no cure for genetic disorders, but some genetic disorders can be treated. Many people with genetic disorders live long, happy lives.

did you know?
A GENETIC MUTATION THAT SHOWS UP IN MORE THAN 1 PERCENT OF THE POPULATION, SUCH AS EYE-COLOR VARIATION, IS CALLED A *POLYMORPHISM*—AN ALTERNATE FORM OF A GENE RATHER THAN AN ABNORMALITY.

CYSTIC FIBROSIS ▼
Cystic fibrosis is a genetic disorder that causes a person's lungs to produce thick mucus. The excess mucus makes breathing difficult and can lead to serious respiratory illnesses. The mucus also blocks the enzymes produced by the pancreas that help digest food. As a result, a person with cystic fibrosis might not be able to absorb enough nutrients from their diet. People with cystic fibrosis used to die in childhood. Now, with better treatments and special diets, they can live much longer lives.

CHROMOSOME 7 ▼
Cystic fibrosis is caused by a mutation in a gene called *CFTR*, located on chromosome 7. The normal gene tells the body how to make a protein that helps keep a healthy balance of salt and water in a person's cells. A person with cystic fibrosis cannot make the healthy protein. He or she has inherited two copies of the abnormal gene, one from each parent.

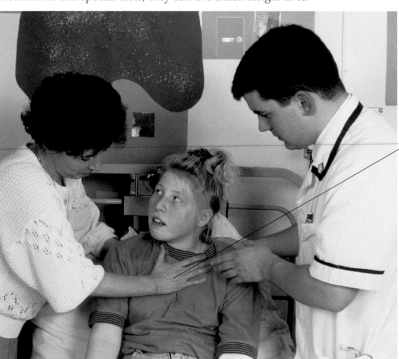

Many people with cystic fibrosis have their chests and backs pounded daily to help loosen mucus in their lungs.

Inheriting a copy of the gene for cystic fibrosis from only one parent does not cause a person to have the disease. However, that person carries the gene. Two carriers have a 25 percent chance of having a child with the disease.

CFTR gene on chromosome 7

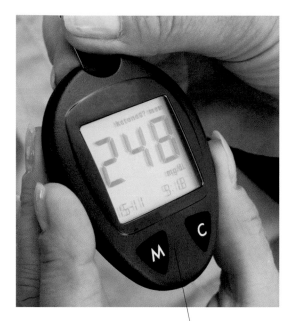

People with diabetes often use a digital monitor to measure the glucose levels in their blood.

Untreated diabetes increases the risk of having poor circulation in the legs and feet. Wounds can't heal without adequate blood circulating to them and can develop gangrene—or dead cells. This sometimes leads to amputation.

DIABETES

Type 1 diabetes is a genetic disorder. About 5–10 percent of Americans diagnosed with diabetes have this type. People with type 1 diabetes do not produce insulin, which is a hormone that's needed for the body to convert food into energy. The body breaks down the food into sugar, called *glucose*, but without insulin, the glucose builds up in the bloodstream instead of becoming available to all the body's cells as energy.

An insulin pen lets the user dial up the correct amount of insulin to be injected.

INSULIN ▶

Type 2 diabetes is not a genetic disorder, but it is much more common than type 1. It can be caused by environmental effects, such as diet and lifestyle choices. In type 2, a person's body cannot produce enough insulin, or the body develops a resistance to insulin. This type can sometimes be controlled with diet or with medication in pill form. If not, people may need the same treatment as those who have type 1 diabetes—injecting themselves with insulin throughout the day.

Insulin is usually injected into the fat of the arms, thighs, or abdomen.

GEOCACHING

Treasure hunting, anyone? Who can resist the opportunity to search for hidden treasure? With the assistance of modern wireless technology, many people are playing a treasure hunting game known as *geocaching* (pronounced *jee oh CASH ing*). Players normally use a handheld Global Positioning System (GPS) device to help locate a hidden "treasure" box called a *geocache*. Geocaching sites on the Internet give players a latitude and longitude, which they enter into the GPS device. The GPS can then show a trail map or compass heading, pointing the way to go. Once there, it is up to the players to pinpoint the treasure's exact location. Each geocache contains a logbook that players sign and usually some items that players take in exchange for items they leave. The development of online communities that link geocachers worldwide adds to the adventure.

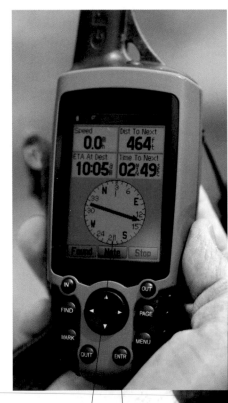

GPS receivers may include a standard magnetic compass that aligns with Earth's magnetic field.

GPS technology is accurate enough to get players within about 30 feet (about 9 m) of the geocache.

◄ HOW GPS WORKS

GPS satellites, in orbit all around Earth, transmit radio waves to your receiver at the speed of light. The receiver measures the time it takes for the satellite's signal to arrive and then can calculate the distance. With information from at least 3 satellites, the receiver can determine the general location of the geocache. The more satellite signals the receiver reads, the more accurately it can pinpoint the position.

HIDING A GEOCACHE ▼

Geocaches are hidden on every continent. Treasure hunters may choose the difficulty of their search. For example, some geocaches are hidden on mountaintops or under water. The geocacher below is carefully placing a geocache into the base of a dead tree. A large container like the one shown may hold multiple "treasures" for geocachers to find. A general rule is that players who take items from a cache replace them with items of their own. Many boxes contain special coins or trackable electronic devices that players carry from one box to another.

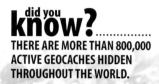

did you know?...............
THERE ARE MORE THAN 800,000 ACTIVE GEOCACHES HIDDEN THROUGHOUT THE WORLD.

GEOCACHE CONTAINERS ▲

Geocaches come in all shapes and sizes. Some are even camouflaged to further challenge players. Because geocaches are placed in the wild for long spans of time, they are usually in weatherized containers that are water and animal resistant.

GEODES

Giant crystals tower overhead. Sparkling crystals cover the walls, ceiling, and floor, surrounding you in glittering color. You are inside a geode! A geode is a hollow rock lined with mineral crystals. A few geodes are big enough to walk into, but most are small enough to hold in your hand. A geode forms in an empty space or pocket within a rock. Hot, mineral-rich water seeps through cracks in igneous rock, for example, depositing layers of microcrystalline minerals on the walls of the opening. These crystals are so tiny you can see them only under a microscope. But as the rock and water cool, larger crystals grow. Geodes can also form in sedimentary rocks, such as limestone. Sometimes the minerals in a geode are replaced by another mineral. Scientists can tell if this has happened because the new mineral has a different crystal shape!

Part of a geode's beauty comes from the layers of different types of minerals that have crystallized inside it.

Traces of iron turn plain quartz into purple amethyst. The purple is often darker near the crystals' tips.

AN ISLAND OF GEODES ▼
Geodes often form within rock that is softer than the minerals that make the geode. When the softer rock weathers away, the geodes remain. Here, on the island of Socotra, in the Indian Ocean, the weathering of soft limestone on this plateau has left behind a field of hard, round geodes.

HIDDEN TREASURES ▼

Opening a geode reveals wonders that have been hidden from view until that very moment. You can crack geodes open with a hammer and chisel or cut them with a special rock saw to reveal more detail. You can also place a geode inside a sock and gently tap it with a hammer. So what's inside? Quartz is the most common geode-forming mineral. In a geode, it can form smooth, milky, banded agate or large, glassy amethyst crystals—or both. Calcite is another common geode-forming mineral. Some geodes contain multiple minerals. For example, calcite crystals can grow on top of quartz, or brass-colored metallic crystals of pyrite can be tucked among the larger crystals. If you have a large geode, try rattling it gently before opening it. You may hear loose crystals inside.

One geode can grow inside another geode. This round calcite geode contains other irregularly shaped calcite geodes.

The crystals in this band of blue agate are submicroscopic—too small to be seen with an ordinary microscope.

The largest crystals, near the center of the geode, were the last to form and took the longest.

GEOLOGIC TIME

A million years may seem like a long time to us, but it is only a tiny fraction of Earth's age. Scientists have calculated Earth to be 4.6 billion years old! Scientists have divided this time into units that we can use to describe the different parts of this immense span of time. To understand the length of Earth's history, imagine how it would look if it were drawn on the face of a clock. Say you mark the beginning of the geologic record of Earth—4.6 billion years ago—at 12:00 on the clock. A full circle of the clock, 12 hours, represents geologic time from the beginning of Earth to the present. In this model, each hour represents about 383 million years. You can use this model to picture the different lengths of time that spanned important events in Earth's history.

A volcano's flow of lava—melted rock from deep underground—gives us an idea of what Earth was like when it first formed.

PRECAMBRIAN: 4.6 BILLION TO 542 MILLION YEARS AGO

Precambrian time is the longest era of the geologic record—more than 10 and one-half hours on the clock model. At the beginning, the planet's surface was mostly melted rock. It eventually cooled and formed a solid crust covered in part by oceans of liquid water. After more than 600 million years—between 1 and 2 hours on the clock—the first living things formed from chemical building blocks in these early oceans. Simple, single-celled bacteria used energy from sunlight and began producing oxygen. This oxygen helped create an atmosphere that would later support more complex life. It was nearly the end of Precambrian time before the first multicelled organisms appeared.

PALEOZOIC: 542 MILLION TO 251 MILLION YEARS AGO

In our clock model, the Paleozoic era took nearly an hour, extending to about 20 minutes after the 11 on the clock. It began with the Cambrian explosion, named for the diversity, or variety, of living things that appeared in that time. The continents came together to form giant land masses that later broke apart. Plants began to grow on land and many kinds of animals evolved. By the end of the Paleozoic, there were forests, amphibians, and reptiles that breathed with lungs. It ended with the largest mass extinction ever: the Permian extinction. About 70 percent of land animals and 90 percent of all ocean species were wiped out.

The oldest known trees had branches and leaves like those of these modern tree ferns.

did you know?
NEARLY 87 PERCENT OF THE PLANET'S 4.6 BILLION-YEAR HISTORY TOOK PLACE BEFORE THE SIMPLEST MULTICELLULAR LIFE FORMS EVEN CAME INTO EXISTENCE.

Modern humans first appeared about 190,000 years ago— less than 2 seconds in the clock model of geologic time!

MESOZOIC: 251 MILLION TO 66 MILLION YEARS AGO

The Mesozoic era lasted for about half an hour on the clock. When you think of extinct animals, you probably think of the dinosaurs. The dinosaurs ruled during this era. However, other living things evolved too. Mammals appeared about 200 million years ago. Birds began to fly about 50 million years after that. Plants also changed. Ferns, then cone-bearing trees, and later flowering plants and trees became the dominant plants on land. The Mesozoic ended with another mass extinction that killed off the dinosaurs. Their absence created an opportunity for modern animals to evolve and flourish.

CENOZOIC: 66 MILLION YEARS AGO TO THE PRESENT

If you imagine that Earth's history took place in a 12-hour period, the entire Cenozoic era happened during only the last 10 minutes. During this era, small mammals and reptiles thrived. As the continents moved closer to where they are today and the climate went through many changes, plants and animals began to evolve with the shifting conditions. Whales evolved from land mammals that moved to the oceans. Grasslands formed where forests retreated. Large grazing animals appeared. Only in the last 30 seconds of the clock model did the ancestors of humans begin to walk on two legs and use tools.

GEORGES BANK

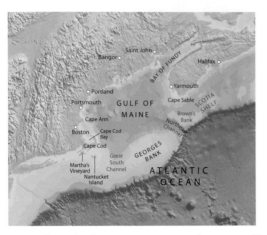

An undersea plateau off the coast of New England, Georges Bank is an oceanographic wonder. More than 100 species of fish live in its nutrient-rich waters. For hundreds of years, Georges Bank has been a highly productive fishing area, but it faces constant threats. Once teeming with sea creatures, Georges Bank has been gutted by overfishing. Many commercial fish species, such as cod, halibut, and haddock, have been nearly eliminated. Large areas of the bank are now off limits to commercial fishing so the numbers of these fish are rising again. Georges Bank is also vulnerable because of another natural resource—oil and natural gas. There could be as much as 1 billion barrels of oil and a rich supply of natural gas beneath the bank. Drillers are pushing hard to get access to it. But environmental activists fear exploration could devastate the sea creature population.

FISHING OUT THE COD ▶
Georges Bank has long been famous for its cod. In the 1800s, Atlantic cod were plentiful and large—from 180 to 210 pounds (about 82 to 95 kg). Now cod are much smaller and far less common. Spawning, or the process of leaving eggs in the water, has increased recently. But the cod still suffers in Georges Bank.

SCALLOP SUCCESS! ▼
The supply of American scallops has increased along the East Coast in recent years, promising good fishing when the scallops mature. Although a scallop can clap its shells together to move away when a predator approaches, it has no defense against a fisherman's net. Fortunately, scallops in Georges Bank are so plentiful that some may die of old age before they can be fished.

LOBSTER TRAPS ▼
Lobsters are bottom-dwelling crustaceans that dine on crabs, clams, and mussels, among other treats. They are fished using traps that pose little threat to the habitat. New limits on *bottom trawling*—dragging a net across the sea floor— have increased the number of lobsters in Georges Bank.

did you know?....................
EUROPEANS FIRST STARTED FISHING GEORGES BANK AROUND THE YEAR 1000, AND TRADED THEIR COD CATCH INTERNATIONALLY.

Walking leg

Claw

Abdomen

Antenna

Tail fin

GEYSERS

What do you get when Mother Earth lets out a steaming burp? A geyser! A geyser is a hot spring that has eruptions. These eruptions send steam and boiling hot water into the air. There are only about 1,000 active geysers on Earth. They are so rare because they form only under very specific conditions. For a geyser to form, there must be a lot of water filling a system of watertight underground cracks. These pipelike cracks must be able to withstand great pressure. Most importantly, this water must be located near a very hot place—such as an underground pocket of melted rock, or magma, that feeds a volcano. Such heat from deep underground is called *geothermal energy*. In nature, geothermal energy powers geysers, many kinds of rock changes, and volcanoes. People use geothermal energy, too. Geothermal power plants are like human-made geysers. The hot steam that comes up can be used to power turbines that generate electricity.

did you know?
THERE ARE MORE GEYSERS WITHIN YELLOWSTONE NATIONAL PARK THAN ANYWHERE ELSE ON EARTH.

OLD FAITHFUL ▼
This reliable geyser erupts every 65 to 92 minutes for a period of 1.5 to 5 minutes. Old Faithful is one of the most frequently erupting of the big geysers in Yellowstone National Park in Wyoming. It sends 3,700–8,400 gallons (about 14,000–31,800 L) of water into the air during each eruption.

Colorful mats of heat-loving bacteria thrive in the hot springs near geysers.

FLY GEYSER ▲
These colorful shapes look like plastic fountains you might see at an amusement park. They are actually rocky mounds deposited by a man-made geyser. In 1964, a company looking for geothermal energy drilled a test well in Nevada. The 200°F (93°C) water was not hot enough for their needs, but after they left, the water kept bubbling up from the ground. Over time, the hot water deposited minerals that built up around the openings in the ground. Various types of heat-loving algae give the rocks their color.

Old Faithful's column of water can shoot as high as 184 feet (about 56 m) in the air.

The rims of hot springs and cones of geysers are made up of deposits of dissolved rock, called *sinter*.

At the surface, the steam rises into the air, followed by the boiling water that has built up. Cooled water seeps back into the ground to begin the process once again.

Pipelike underground cracks

Water heated by hot rocks forms bubbles of water vapor, which can be trapped in narrow passageways.

Hot spring

HOW A GEYSER WORKS ▲

The boiling point of a substance increases with pressure. Water deep underground is at high pressure due to the weight of the water above. So this water must reach temperatures higher than 212°F (100°C) to boil. Once this water starts to boil, bubbles of water vapor travel up toward the surface. These bubbles get trapped in the narrow passageways. As more bubbles are trapped, the force on the water above increases until a small amount of water is pushed out of the geyser. Once this water is out of the way, there is less pressure on the water underneath. Less pressure means the water will boil at a lower temperature—one it has already reached. All of the water boils at once, sending steam and hot water erupting out of the geyser.

GIANT MAMMALS

The last 65 million years are known as the Cenozoic era. This era is also known as the Age of Mammals, because mammals thrived during this time. Many mammals grew to incredible sizes during the Cenozoic era. These giant mammals included beavers almost the size of modern day black bears, and cave lions that weighed around 800 pounds (360 kg)! Most giant mammals became extinct around 10,000 years ago for reasons that are still being debated. Some scientists believe early humans hunted the giant mammals to extinction. Other scientists blame the last ice age, which began 70,000 years ago when glaciers—large, moving sheets of ice—spread across much of Earth limiting greatly the resources these animals needed to survive.

WOOLLY MAMMOTH ▶

The woolly mammoth—a symbol of the last ice age—is probably the most famous Cenozoic mammal. Scientists know a lot about them from preserved mammoth carcasses found in Siberia and from European cave drawings. Woolly mammoths dominated the cold, northern regions of Europe, Asia, and North America between 350,000 and 10,000 years ago. They were about 11 feet (about 3 m) tall and may have eaten about 300 pounds (136 kg) of vegetation a day!

A two-layered coat kept mammoths toasty warm. Long, shaggy guard hairs covered a layer of dense underfur.

Woolly mammoths had curving ivory tusks that could reach lengths of 10 feet (about 3 m).

did you know?

THE NOW EXTINCT HORNLESS RHINOCEROS *INDRICOTHERIUM* WAS THE LARGEST LAND MAMMAL EVER! IT WAS 26 FEET (ALMOST 8 M) LONG, 18 FEET (ABOUT 5.5 M) TALL, AND WEIGHED ABOUT 20 TONS.

A mammoth stands 11 feet tall; this man is 5'9" tall.

ARSINOITHERIUM ►

This rhinoceros-like African herbivore lived in swamps around 30 million years ago. A male arsinoitherium had two huge horns sticking out from the front of its head. These horns were hollow and scientists believe they may have been used to produce mating calls and to duel with other males. These massive mammals stood about 6 feet (1.8 m) at the shoulder.

The giant sloth's head was small compared with its body.

Arsinoitherium stands about 6 feet tall; this man is 5'9" tall.

◄ GIANT SLOTH

The king of the Cenozoic ground sloths was the South American mammal *Megatherium*. As big as a modern elephant, the long-haired *Megatherium* resembled an overgrown guinea pig with a long tail. Many scientists think that *Megatherium* could stand on its hind legs and dine on leaves and twigs that it pulled off the very top branches of trees with its long, sharp claws.

A giant sloth stands 20 feet tall; this man is 5'9" tall.

Megatherium may have used its strong tail for balance and support when it stood on its back legs to reach leaves.

GILA MONSTER

Despite their name, Gila monsters (pronounced *HEE la*) are not cold-blooded killers . . . but they are cold-blooded reptiles. Actually, Gila monsters are ectothermic, which means they cannot control their internal body temperature. Like other reptiles, they are dependent on the temperature of their surroundings and have to bask in the sun to keep warm. This warmth gives them energy to hunt, scavenge, and search for mates. When it is warm, they hunt at night for small mammals, frogs, and their favorite food—birds' eggs. When it gets too hot outside, Gila monsters escape to their cool, underground burrows. In the winter, Gilas hibernate in their burrows. Gila monsters are one of two known species of venomous lizards in North America. They live in the deserts of the southwestern United States and northern Mexico.

VENOMOUS BITE ▶

Gila monsters use muscular jaws and sharp, curved teeth to clamp down on their prey. Their venom flows into the victim through grooves in the lizards' teeth. Gila monsters will often latch onto their victims and refuse to let go! This gives the venom a chance to seep in and weaken the prey. Though painful, Gila monster bites are rarely deadly to humans.

Flat, triangular head

The Gila uses its forked tongue to "smell" and track prey.

Gilas are not very fast and must sneak up on their prey.

PROTECTIVE BUMPS ▲

Gila monsters are beautifully colored animals with black and yellow, pink, or orange markings. The Gila's patterned skin helps it blend into desert shadows, while the bright colors may advertise its venomous nature and warn predators to stay away. Though most lizard scales are flat and overlapping, Gila monsters are covered with bumpy, nonoverlapping scales that protect the lizard when it climbs up trees and cactuses in search of food.

Gilas do not chew. They use their large mouth to swallow food whole.

Venom glands near the front of the lower jaw

The oversized tail stores fat.

Each of the five toes on the Gila's foot contain sharp claws for digging burrows and uncovering eggs.

did you know?..................
SCIENTISTS USED A PROTEIN IN GILA MONSTER SALIVA TO DEVELOP A DRUG THAT TREATS DIABETES.

BIG FELLA ▼

Gila monsters are squat, thick-bodied lizards with short, muscular legs. They store fat in their large, chunky tails and feed off the fat stores throughout the winter. Gila monsters can reach lengths of 2 feet (0.6 m) and weigh more than 5 pounds (about 2.3 kg), making them the largest lizard native to North America!

Gila monsters have poor eyesight. They use their senses of smell and taste to hunt.

GLACIERS

Earth's poles are locked in ice, but for how long? Glaciers—large masses of ice that grow and move over time—have advanced and retreated throughout Earth's history. As they do, they leave behind telltale landforms as signs of their movement. Deposits of rock left by glaciers in South Africa and Australia, which are 290 million years old, provide evidence that these areas that are now separate were once joined. At that time, much of the world was covered in ice sheets. During the reign of the dinosaurs, 145 million years ago, the world was warmer. There were no ice sheets on Earth, not even at the poles! Sea levels were higher and a shallow inland sea covered what is now the Great Plains of the United States. Cooler temperatures eventually returned, glaciers formed again, and sea levels fell. Today, three fourths of Earth's fresh water is frozen in ice caps and glaciers. As Earth's average temperature rises, glacier ice melts faster than it accumulates. Will shallow inland seas return some day?

CAVES AND CALVING ▼

Glacier ice can be unstable where a glacier meets the sea. The vertical cracks, called *crevasses*, in this glacier form at areas of weakness. Meltwater, running down into a crevasse, has widened one crack far below into an ice cave. Often, huge chunks of the glacier break free and fall into the sea below becoming icebergs. This process, called *calving*, increases as global temperatures rise.

did you know?
THE GLACIER ICE IN ANTARCTICA IS MORE THAN 2.5 MILES (4 KM) THICK!

Accumulation zone, where snow builds up from winter to winter

Glacier's end, called its *terminus*

◄ A GLACIER FORMS

Glaciers form when snow falls and stays frozen from one winter until the next. Each year, more snow accumulates, making a larger snowfield that reflects the summer sunlight. Reflected sunlight reduces the amount of melting before winter arrives again. Years of accumulation, along with melting and recrystallizing of snow, creates a mass of ice that advances downhill under its own weight—a glacier.

A medial, or middle, moraine forms where two glaciers flow together, joining their lateral moraines.

Lateral, or side, moraines form terraces along the valley's edge.

A glacier fills the valley.

Meltwater lakes

Meltwater streams

Crevasses can fill with sediment washed in by meltwater.

Lateral moraine

Meltwater chamber

A moraine is a pile of sediment left by a melting or moving glacier.

The terminal moraine is the farthest moraine left by the end, or snout, of a glacier.

PICK UP AND DROP OFF ▲

Glaciers are powerful agents of erosion and deposition. As they grow, glaciers pick up pieces of sediment ranging in size from boulders the size of cars to dust as fine as flour. These sediments scour the land when the glacier moves. They gouge grooves in bedrock and widen valley walls. Where the glacier melts, it drops its load, forming distinctive landforms, called *moraines*, that persist long after the glacier is gone.

GLASS

People have been making glass for thousands of years. The earliest known glass objects were beads, made by Egyptians around 3,500 B.C. In about 27 B.C., Syrians learned they could insert a long metal tube into molten glass and blow into it to create hollow glass containers, such as vases and bottles. Glass is an unusual material. When it is a hot, molten liquid, it can be formed into shapes. Then it hardens into a transparent solid but still retains some properties of a liquid. When most substances are solid, the molecules are like tightly packed bricks in a wall. The molecules of liquids are farther apart, allowing light to pass through. This is why most liquids are clear or semi-clear and most solids are opaque. Glass has properties of both liquids and solids. The molecules in a glass window, for example, do not move, but are far enough apart to allow light to pass through.

did you know?
TO MAKE A WINDOWPANE, MOLTEN GLASS IS POURED ON TOP OF MOLTEN TIN. THE LIQUID GLASS FLOATS AND SPREADS INTO A SMOOTH, EVEN LAYER.

MAKING LIQUID GLASS ▼
People make glass by melting pure sand with other minerals in a furnace heated to 3,092°F (1,700°C). They add soda ash to lower the melting point—the temperature at which solids become liquid. Limestone is added to increase the strength and stability of the glass. Adding broken pieces of other glass speeds up the melting process. Ingredients such as copper, gold, and other chemical elements give glass a variety of colors.

72 percent sand

The remaining 5 percent can include chemicals that affect the color of the glass. Iron oxide is used in green or brown glass. Crystal glass and television glass contain barium carbonate.

15 percent soda ash (sodium carbonate)

8 percent limestone (calcium carbonate)

◄ GLASS BLOWING

A glassworker winds the glass, in its liquid state, onto a long, hollow iron rod and blows a bubble of air into the glass to give it a pear shape. Then, the worker rolls the iron rod shaping the glass. Last, the glass blower reheats the glass and blows more air into it to give the object its final shape.

Blue glass

Patterned glass

Green glass

It takes a worker years of practice to know when glass is the right consistency to blow and shape.

A glass blower shapes glass into a vase.

THE COLORS OF GLASS ▲

Cobalt turns glass dark blue, while gold can make glass ruby red. A small amount of chromium turns glass emerald green. Glass made from beach sand is usually light green or blue, since beach sand often has impurities, such as iron, in it. Lead makes glass sparkle and reflect.

GLIDING

Moving through the air propelled by a force that is actively pulling or pushing you forward—the force provided by an airplane engine, for example—is called *flying.* Sailing along without such a force is called *gliding.* Like fliers, gliders depend on a force called *lift,* which is created when a bird or airplane moves through air molecules at a high enough speed. Wing shapes are designed to take advantage of this lifting force by bending the air that flows over and under them in different ways. Airplanes achieve lift as they speed down the runway at 100 miles per hour (about 161 km/h). Gliders, on the other hand, have only the initial launch to provide forward motion—after that, they must rely on other forces. Birds fly by flapping their wings, but most birds glide when they travel long distances. Because they are not flapping their wings, they don't expend much energy.

3 A gliding bird rises in circles around the warm air currents.

4 When the air cools and stops rising, the bird circling the thermal peels off and eventually glides downward.

2 A bird takes advantage of thermals by spreading its wings to let the rising air carry it higher and higher with little effort.

1 Thermal currents, shown as red arrows, are columns of air that rise when the sun heats the ground below them.

SILENT SOARING ▶
Gliders like this barn owl are also lifted higher by thermal currents, also called *thermals.* Owl feathers are specially adapted for flying silently. Their flight feathers are coated with fluffy down feathers that muffle sound so they can quietly glide in and swoop up their prey.

 **THE LONGEST PARAGLIDE LASTED MORE THAN 11 HOURS.**

▼ PARAGLIDING ABOVE TURKEY

A paraglider—called a *pilot*—runs down a gentle hill, pulling a cloth wing against the air as if it were a kite. The wing lifts the pilot. Once aloft, by catching thermals, paragliders can stay up for several hours, soar to heights of 15,000 feet (almost 4.6 km), and cover great distances. Lines that connect the harness to the wing enable the pilot to steer and control the speed.

SWOOPING COLUGOS ▲

"Flying lemurs" do not fly, nor are they lemurs. They are mammals from Asia, also called *colugos,* that jump from trees and can glide the length of two football fields. They use flaps of skin that stretch around their bodies from fingers to toes to tail. The remarkable design of their skin flaps allows them to make swift ninety-degree turns. The colugo shown here is gliding while her young one holds on!

GLOBAL WARMING

On a cold night, a blanket keeps you warm. In cold space, greenhouse gases like carbon dioxide (CO_2) and methane surround Earth and keep it warm. When the sun's rays enter the atmosphere, Earth's surface absorbs most of the heat; the rest radiates back into the atmosphere. Some of this radiated heat passes into space, but greenhouse gases trap most of it. Living things need a certain amount of this trapped warmth to survive. Burning fossil fuels—oil, coal, and natural gas—to power automobiles, factories, and homes releases substantial amounts of CO_2 into the atmosphere. Most scientists are confident that these CO_2 emissions increase the amount of greenhouse gas in the atmosphere, trapping too much thermal radiation. They have concluded that global warming—the increase in Earth's average surface temperature—leads to climate change that impacts life on Earth.

MELTING ICE ▼

Studies show that global warming is changing circulation patterns in the oceans and atmosphere. These changes, along with warming temperatures, contribute to the widespread melting and shrinking of glaciers. Scientists use satellite images and computer models to observe and predict changes in the rate of melting. Evidence indicates that glacial melting is accelerating. Melting arctic ice reduces the habitat of wildlife, such as polar bears.

did you know?..........................
MORE THAN HALF OF ALL FOSSIL FUELS EVER USED HAVE BEEN CONSUMED IN JUST THE LAST 20 YEARS.

RISING SEA LEVELS ►

Global warming is causing sea levels to rise faster, partly because of the rapidly melting glaciers. At the same time, warmer water temperatures increase the volume of ocean water. This process is called *thermal expansion*. Average sea levels are expected to rise by 7 to 23 inches (about 18 to 58 cm) or more by the end of this century. Barrier islands and coastal wetlands may be lost, and coastal communities are at greater risk of flooding. The streets of Venice, Italy—a city historically prone to flooding—have some degree of flooding 200 days per year. If sea levels rise, that number could rise.

KEY
Land submerged if sea level rises

13-FOOT (ABOUT 4-M) RISE IN SEA LEVEL

Rising sea levels in Florida would affect cities and ecosystems.

26-FOOT (ABOUT 8-M) RISE IN SEA LEVEL

Much of southern Florida, including Miami, would be submerged if sea levels rose 26 feet (about 8 m).

Researchers are developing gates that will close Venice's three inlets against the flooding tides of the Adriatic Sea.

◄ BLACK CARBON POLLUTION

Incomplete combustion, or partial burning, of fossil fuels, biofuels, and biomass, such as wood, releases black carbon into the atmosphere. Black carbon is a type of tiny floating particle called an *aerosol*. Black carbon absorbs incoming solar radiation and contributes to atmospheric warming. Researchers estimate that, in the past 30 years, aerosols have caused 45 percent of the warming in the Arctic region.

GOLD MINING

You see bits of bright, shiny metal in a rock. You've struck gold! But how do you get the gold away from the rock that surrounds it? Gold is a mineral, usually found in a mixture with other minerals, such as quartz. It is also a single element, like iron, that you see on the periodic table. Gold does not react easily with other substances—oxygen doesn't corrode it, for example—and that quality is part of what makes it so valuable, in addition to the fact that it is rare. You can extract, or separate, gold from its mixture of minerals in a variety of ways. Gold is one of the heaviest elements, so gold miners can sift a mixture of crushed rock and water to get gold to sink to the bottom. Another way to extract gold is to add liquid mercury to a mixture of gold and rocks or sand. The mercury forms a type of mixture with the gold. Sifting separates out the rocks and sand. Using heat or chemicals, the gold is separated from the mercury.

Dirt from tunnels

HARD ROCK MINING ▲

Some gold occurs in large deposits in underground rock. Workers dig mine shafts—or tunnels—that let them move gold-containing rock, called *ore*, out of the mine. The ore is carried by trucks or carts that travel to and from the surface. Above ground, the gold is separated from the rock. The rock that no longer contains gold is taken back underground and used to refill old mine shafts.

Tunnel support

Mine shaft

Mining trucks

Oxygen supply

Lift to take workers up and down the mine shaft

SHAPING GOLD ▶

Part of the reason that gold is so desirable is that it is a soft metal—about as easy to dent or scratch as a penny. One way to distinguish a nugget of real gold from other yellow, shiny rocks is to test its hardness. Other minerals that look like gold, such as iron pyrite, also called *fool's gold*, are much harder. Pure gold can easily be hammered into very thin sheets, called *gold leaf*, and used to decorate buildings or statues. It can be made into extremely thin wire and used in electronics. Gold can also be melted and poured into molds to make rings and other shapes.

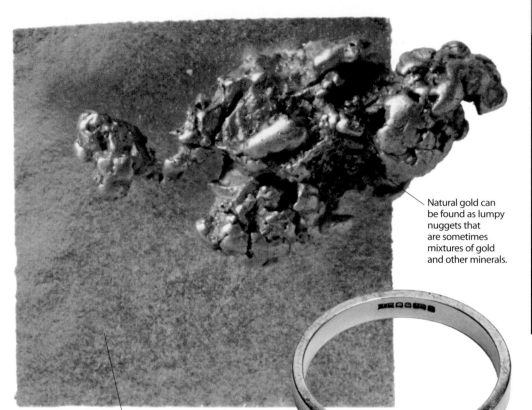

Natural gold can be found as lumpy nuggets that are sometimes mixtures of gold and other minerals.

Gold leaf is only a few hundred atoms thick—or about 500 times thinner than a piece of aluminum foil.

Units called *karats* indicate how much of an alloy, a type of metal mixture, is pure gold. On a scale where 24 karats is the highest purity, this 9-karat gold ring is 9 parts gold and 15 parts other metals.

did you know?....................

ALL OF THE WORLD'S MINED GOLD WOULD FIT IN A WAREHOUSE THE SIZE OF A FOOTBALL FIELD AND SHORTER THAN A ONE-STORY BUILDING.

Quartz is the most abundant mineral on Earth.

Gold is one of the rarest minerals on Earth.

◀ GOLD VEIN IN QUARTZ

Pure gold can form layers between other minerals, such as quartz. This layer is called a *vein* or *lode deposit*. There are various ways in which gold deposits form. Scientists think that a gold vein can form when underground water is heated by molten rock deep beneath Earth's surface and dissolves metal from the rocks. When the heated water cools, it leaves behind a gold deposit. Erosion by a river or rainwater can wash away bits of rock and gold from a vein. These bits may pile up downstream, creating a placer deposit. Gold mining techniques vary depending on the type of gold deposit.

GORILLAS

Gorillas are members of a group of primates known as the great apes. This group includes gorillas, chimpanzees, orangutans, and humans. Great apes are distinguished from monkeys by their larger size, upright posture, and lack of tails. Primates shared a common ancestor that lived more than 65 million years ago, but the gorilla line began only about 7 million years ago. Today, scientists recognize the several subspecies of gorilla, all living in equatorial Africa: the western lowland gorilla, the eastern lowland gorilla, and the mountain gorilla. Like all primates, gorillas have highly developed brains and a great capacity for learning. Researchers have taught gorillas sign language, which the gorillas have used to identify objects, numbers, words, and people. Researchers have also documented gorillas using sticks and stumps as tools in the wild. And, thanks to the work of dedicated scientists such as Dian Fossey, we also know a great deal about gorilla communication. These amazing animals express themselves using complicated vocalizations and gestures, including hoots, whines, chest beating, lip puckering, and smiling.

▲ SNOWFLAKE, THE WHITE GORILLA

Snowflake, a beautiful and rare white gorilla, was the first ape with a documented case of albinism. Albinism, which can also affect humans, is a genetic mutation that prevents the production of melanin—the pigment that colors our eyes, hair, and skin.

Older male eastern lowland gorillas are called "silverbacks" because their black hair turns silver below their shoulders.

Gorilla nose prints are like human fingerprints! Scientists can use them to identify individual gorillas.

Gorillas have five toes, including an opposable big toe that helps them grab branches and objects with their feet.

GORILLA REPRODUCTION ▶

Gorillas have large, round bellies, making it difficult for scientists to determine whether a female is pregnant. Female gorillas give birth to one 4.5-pound (about 2 kg) infant gorilla after an 8½-month pregnancy. After about 4 years, she will give birth again. Young gorillas grow twice as fast as human babies and become independent when they are about 3½ years old!

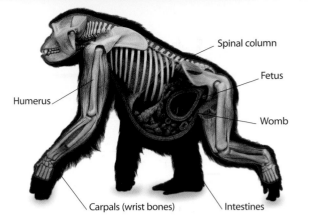

Spinal column

Fetus

Humerus

Womb

Carpals (wrist bones)

Intestines

PARENTAL CARE ▶

Gorilla mothers invest a lot of energy in raising and protecting their young. For its first 5 months, a young gorilla never leaves its mother's side. The mother is responsible for feeding, grooming, and nesting with her offspring. The father teaches the young gorilla to interact and play with the rest of the troop.

Gorillas have binocular, color vision that lets them focus both eyes on an object and judge distance.

At about 6 or 7 months of age, young gorillas ride piggyback. They hang on by clutching their mother's long hair.

Unlike monkeys, apes do not have tails.

When gorillas walk, they use their arms (which are longer than their legs) for support, pressing their third and fourth knuckles against the ground. This is why they are known as "knuckle walkers."

◀ WESTERN LOWLAND GORILLAS

These gorillas live in the rain forests of central Africa and, like all gorillas, are highly endangered as a result of habitat destruction and poaching. Western lowland gorillas are distinguished by a wide, cone-shaped head, small ears, and short hair. They are shy vegetarians who use their strong jaws to eat more than 200 different types of plants. Male gorillas can eat up to 45 pounds (about 20.4 kg) of food per day!

GPS TRACKING

Birds with backpacks? Toads wearing tiny belts? These and other Global Positioning System (GPS) units make it easier to track an animal's location. Tiny units are attached to collars on moose, glued to bat wings, and swallowed by fish. Researchers used to attach radio transmitters to wildlife, and then fly over an area to follow the signal. Now, GPS receivers record the animal's location every 15 minutes, and the researcher does not have to be nearby. A radio transmitter may be added to the GPS unit to transmit data about the animal's movements periodically or to help researchers locate the device when they go to retrieve it. Many devices are capable of sending data to a remote computer using satellites or cellphone networks.

FIND THAT RUNAWAY! ▼

Wandering pets can be tracked using GPS. Dog owners can attach units weighing less than an egg to their pets. The unit can locate the dog and transmit that location to a cellphone. Owners of guide dogs can speak their destination into a handheld GPS device, which communicates with another device attached to the guide dog's handle. The handle vibrates to signal each turn to the owner!

A GPS receiver pinpoints its location in relation to GPS satellites that are orbiting Earth.

◄ AN ELEPHANT IN A HAYSTACK

You might think that keeping track of something as large as an elephant is easy, but it's not! Because of the vast areas of wilderness that form an elephant's range, the task is almost impossible without the aid of technology. An African-based conservation charity, Save the Elephants, tracks individual elephants with GPS. The data are combined with satellite imagery, allowing scientists to follow the animals' journeys in real time.

did you know?

SOLAR CELLS ARE USED TO POWER GPS UNITS FOR TRACKING LONG-DISTANCE BIRD MIGRATIONS.

PRESERVING A SPECIES ▲

Oriental white storks are adored in Japan, but they have been extinct in the wild there since the early 1970s. It took many years to learn how to breed the storks in captivity, but eventually five were released into the wild in 2005. The precious birds were fitted with lightweight GPS tracking devices that help scientists monitor their movements. These efforts should help restore this highly endangered species to the wild.

GRAVITRON

The carnival ride starts to spin faster and you feel yourself pressing against the wall behind you. You seem to be getting heavier. It's hard to pull your arms away from the padded wall. Suddenly, the floor drops away! You are sure you will fall, but you just keep spinning. The Gravitron is a popular carnival ride that uses a force known as *centripetal force* to give you a thrill. An object keeps moving in a straight line unless a net force acts on it. When you are whirling in a Gravitron, you have a net force acting on you that causes you to move in a circular path rather than flinging you in a straight line. That force is centripetal force. This same force keeps the moon and satellites in near-circular, or elliptical, orbits. In this case, gravity is pulling these bodies toward Earth's center. In the Gravitron, the wall you are pressed against allows centripetal force to keep you in your orbit!

RIDING THE GRAVITRON ▶

In a Gravitron ride, you feel as if you are being pushed against the wall, but the force is really just the opposite. If the wall were not there, you and your fellow passengers would fly off the ride the way a baseball flies out of a pitcher's hand.

The momentum of the moving disk keeps the gyroscope at the same angle. It takes a lot of force to change the motion.

GYROSCOPE ▲

A *gyroscope* is a device with a disk that spins rapidly about its axis. Gyroscopes are useful for studying the forces of circular motion, and they have important applications in air, sea, and land navigation. They are also used in the International Space Station and the Space Shuttle to maintain correct orientations.

did you know? RIDERS ON THE GRAVITRON MOVE AROUND IN A CIRCLE AT ABOUT 40 MILES PER HOUR (ABOUT 64 KM/H).

Path planet would take if
there were no gravity

Planet following an
elliptical orbit around star

Acceleration toward
star due to pull of gravity

Comet from
deep space

Star

Planet following
a more eccentric
(less circular) orbit

A comet's
hyperbolic path

In this ride, the centripetal force is three
times the force of gravity. Astronauts
train in similar rides that have a
centripetal force almost seven
times as strong.

◄ HOLDING ONTO THE PLANETS

Planets moving around a star are held
in place by centripetal force. That force
is created by gravity. Without gravity, the
planet's inertia, or tendency to keep moving
in a straight line, would cause it to fly away
into space. The mass of the star constantly
pulls the planet inward. If inertia is greater
than the pull toward the star, an object such
as a comet does not orbit, but instead follows
a hyperbolic path, which is elongated and
not a closed curve. The comet eventually
leaves the star far behind.

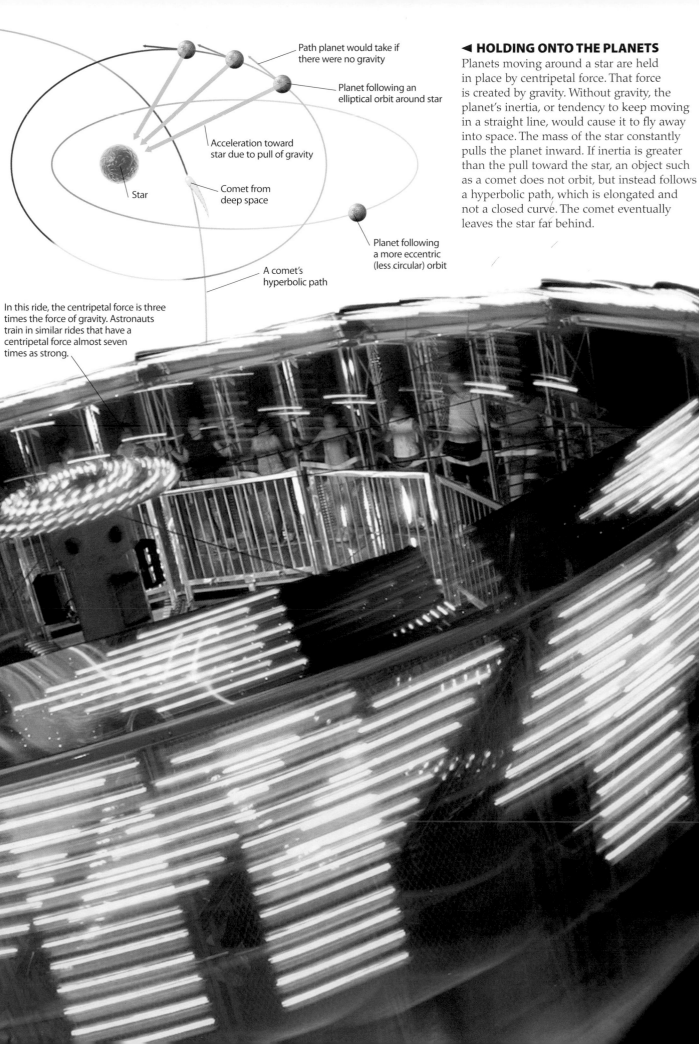

GRAVITY

No matter where you stand on Earth's surface, gravity pulls you toward the center of the planet. As you stand, the ground is pushing upward on your feet in reaction to the gravitational force. In deep space, where the gravitational pull of stars and planets is very small, astronauts experience a sense of weightlessness, a condition called *microgravity*. It's possible to feel this sensation on Earth, if only for a short time during a jump off the ground. You can feel reduced gravity by taking a fast elevator ride down in a tall building. If you jump inside the elevator, it takes longer than usual to come to the floor because the elevator is falling, too.

SCIENCE IN SPACE ▼

The International Space Station is constantly being pulled toward Earth by gravity. Everything inside the station is being pulled at the same rate. This creates a condition of microgravity that is ideal for scientific experiments. In Earth's gravity, less dense, hot gases and soot from a candle flame rise. The soot gives the flame its yellow color. Cooler, denser gases sink, bringing oxygen to the base of the flame. In microgravity, the flame spreads in every direction, because there is no force moving the gases. Very little oxygen moves to the flame, so the flame's temperature drops. The cooler flame produces very little soot, so it burns blue.

Space scientists study the growth of substances, such as these salt crystals, in microgravity to learn more about the properties of materials.

did you
know?...........................
WANT TO BE TALLER? SPEND TIME IN
MICROGRAVITY. WHEN THERE IS NO
DOWNWARD PRESSURE ON THE SPINE,
ASTRONAUTS BECOME ALMOST 2 INCHES
(5 CM) TALLER.

THE FLOATING SCIENTIST ▲

Astronauts inside the space station are being pulled by gravity
at exactly the same rate as the station itself, so they don't fall to
the floor. They train for orbit in large jet airplanes that fly up and
down in curving paths. The plane, known as the Vomit Comet,
and its contents are falling at the same rate for about 25 seconds,
simulating microgravity. Physicist Stephen Hawking, floating
above, experienced microgravity during this type of flight.

▲ COMING DOWN TO EARTH

As the motocross rider jumps from the ramp, his
muscles provide a force that moves him upward.
Once he is in the air, the force of gravity takes over
and he falls. During the jump, the boy and the
bike fall at the same rate, so he experiences a brief
feeling of weightlessness. During that time, he can
perform a trick called a *cordova* while doing a back
flip, and land—all in a fraction of a second.

GREAT LAKES

When the last ice age ended and Earth began to warm, a thick continental ice sheet, or glacier, retreated toward Canada across the area we know as the Great Lakes region. The glacier was so powerful and heavy that it tore away rocks and soil as it moved, gouging out huge basins in Earth's surface. Glacial meltwater filled these early lakebeds. Over thousands of years these primitive lakes evolved into the Great Lakes we know today. The Great Lakes watershed, which is a large area of land that holds and drains all the water above and below ground, is the largest system of fresh surface water in the world. The watershed consists of five large lakes—Superior, Michigan, Huron, Erie, and Ontario—plus one small one, Lake St. Clair. It also includes four connecting rivers, or channels—St. Marys, St. Clair, Detroit, and Niagara—plus the St. Lawrence Seaway, which carries the water to the Atlantic Ocean.

Lake Ontario, with the city of Toronto on its shore, has the smallest surface area of the Great Lakes, at about 7,389 square miles (about 19,000 km^2). It has an average depth of about 280 feet (86 m).

The Great Lakes watershed stretches into eight states—Illinois, Indiana, Michigan, Minnesota, New York, Ohio, Pennsylvania, and Wisconsin—and two Canadian provinces—Ontario and Quebec.

Superior

Huron

Michigan

Ontario

Erie

CYCLES AND SEASONS

Even though water cycles continuously from Earth's surface into the atmosphere and back, there is seasonal variation in the rate. The water level in the Great Lakes decreases during the fall and early winter, when cool air above the warm water increases evaporation. In the spring, evaporation slows, while snowmelt runoff and precipitation increase lake levels.

HUMAN IMPACT ▶

Recreational users of the Great Lakes have to compete with other users. City, farm, and industrial wastes sometimes flow into parts of the ecosystem. Precipitation carries pollutants to the expansive lake surfaces. These pollutants remain in the lakes and become concentrated. When they enter the food chain and water supply, they become a health concern.

did you know? ....
THE GREAT LAKES CONTAIN ABOUT 20 PERCENT OF EARTH'S FRESH SURFACE WATER AND ABOUT 95 PERCENT OF THE U.S. SUPPLY.

THE LAKE EFFECT ▼

The Great Lakes are big enough to cause a weather phenomenon called the *lake effect*. In fall and winter, the lake water cools more slowly than the surrounding land does. When a mass of cold arctic air flows over the vast expanse of warmer water, heat and water vapor rise into the cold air mass. The water vapor condenses and forms clouds, which drop their lake effect snow when the wind carries them over the shore.

Shipping, manufacturing, tourism, and recreation are major industries in the Great Lakes region. Large cities put large demands on the water.

GUITAR

A guitar's strings vibrate when you pluck, pick, or strum them. When you hear the sound, you know it is coming from a guitar—not a violin or a piano. An instrument's vibrations are waves of particular frequencies, the number of waves that occur in a certain period of time. Each note an instrument plays has a certain tone, called its *fundamental tone*. When you hear that tone from a guitar, which comes from a wave moving up and down a string, you are also hearing other tones, called *overtones*, that are characteristic of a guitar. The frequencies of the overtones are related to the fundamental tone mathematically—they are twice, three times, or another multiple of the frequency of the fundamental tone. You hear the sound as one note, but it is harmonious and musical because of its overtones.

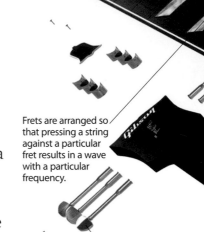

Tuning posts to hold strings at top

Frets are arranged so that pressing a string against a particular fret results in a wave with a particular frequency.

Tuning peg, to adjust tension of string

Neck

◀ UNPLUGGED
The strings of an acoustic guitar—one that is not electric—make the bridge vibrate. The bridge is the piece to which the strings are attached at the bottom. The bridge is attached to the flat front of the guitar—the piece with a hole in it—called the *soundboard*. The vibration of the strings transfers to the soundboard and then to the air inside the guitar, amplifying the sound.

did you know? A GUITAR CAN HAVE AS FEW AS 4 OR AS MANY AS 18 STRINGS.

Bridge

Soundboard

Pick guard

MUSICAL NOTATION ▲
Music is written on a framework of five lines, called a *staff* or *pentagram*. Notes are marked on the lines and spaces corresponding to the particular sound to be played. Notes are labeled A through G, and then back to A. The space from one A to the next A, or B to B, is called an *octave*. Written music is like a written language that uses notes instead of words.

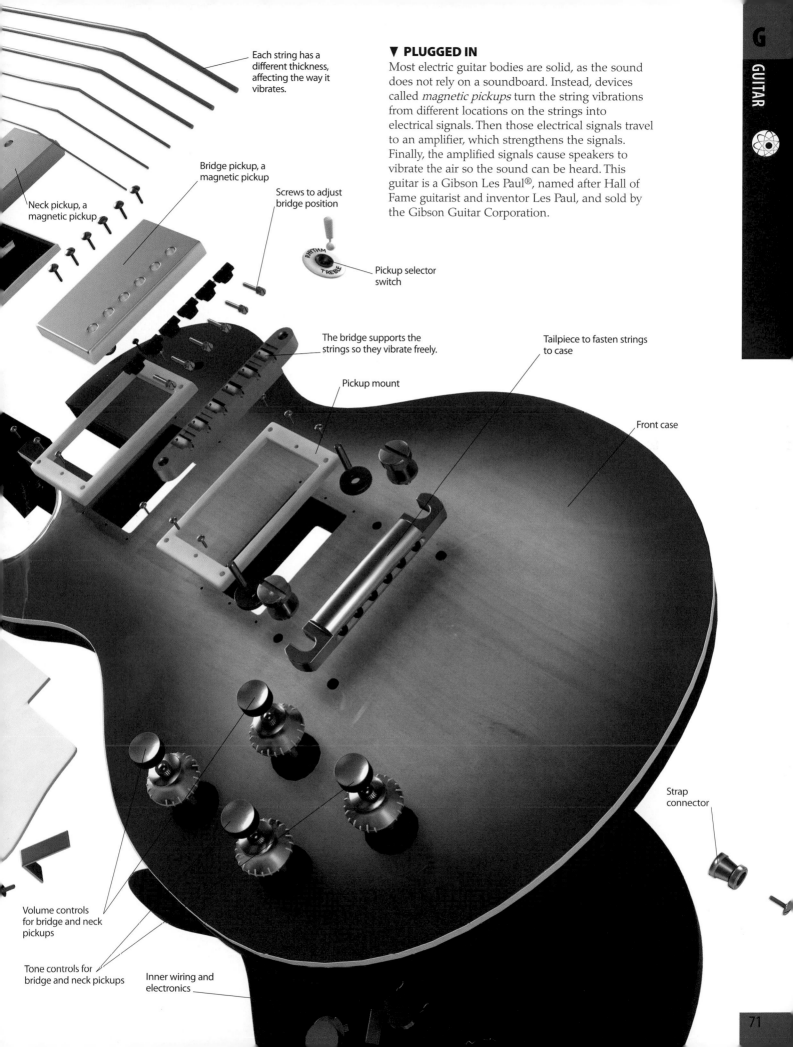

Each string has a
different thickness,
affecting the way it
vibrates.

▼ PLUGGED IN

Most electric guitar bodies are solid, as the sound
does not rely on a soundboard. Instead, devices
called *magnetic pickups* turn the string vibrations
from different locations on the strings into
electrical signals. Then those electrical signals travel
to an amplifier, which strengthens the signals.
Finally, the amplified signals cause speakers to
vibrate the air so the sound can be heard. This
guitar is a Gibson Les Paul®, named after Hall of
Fame guitarist and inventor Les Paul, and sold by
the Gibson Guitar Corporation.

Bridge pickup, a
magnetic pickup

Screws to adjust
bridge position

Neck pickup, a
magnetic pickup

Pickup selector
switch

The bridge supports the
strings so they vibrate freely.

Tailpiece to fasten strings
to case

Pickup mount

Front case

Strap
connector

Volume controls
for bridge and neck
pickups

Tone controls for
bridge and neck pickups

Inner wiring and
electronics

HAZARDOUS MATERIALS

Chemicals are used in many ways all around you. They are used to purify water in swimming pools, feed crops in farm fields, and clear the clogged pipes in homes. Some chemicals are very dangerous, and even in the small quantities you can find at home or in a lab, they must be handled carefully. Every place that uses hazardous chemicals has a *Material Safety Data Sheet* (MSDS) for each chemical. This sheet contains all of the known information about the dangers of the substance, and tells how to handle spills. It's very likely that your school has many MSDS forms on file that can be found easily in case of an emergency.

This diamond-shaped label was designed to tell anyone using, shipping, or cleaning up a spill exactly what hazards to watch for. Each of the four sections gives specific information about the material.

Fire hazard levels range from 0 (will not burn) to 4 (extremely flammable).

Health hazard levels range from 0 (no danger to health) to 4 (can cause death).

Reactivity hazard levels range from 0 (stable) to 4 (easily detonates)

Special hazards tell of other dangers to watch for like materials that react violently with water (W) or are acidic (ACID).

3 **2** **0** **W**

BIOLOGICAL HAZARDS ▼

Biohazards that affect humans are organic in origin and are caused by materials such as viruses, bacteria, plants, and animals. Different symbols were used to indicate different kinds of biological hazards until the international biohazard symbol was adopted.

⚠ CAUTION

Biohazard

KEEPING PEOPLE SAFE ►

Workers at hospitals and research labs routinely handle biohazards. This researcher wears a suit inflated with filtered air to protect him from the Ebola virus. Any lab work requires eye protection because eyes are especially vulnerable to damage. His suit keeps contaminants from being carried home at the end of the shift. Specific kinds of protective gloves are designed to protect against particular types of hazards.

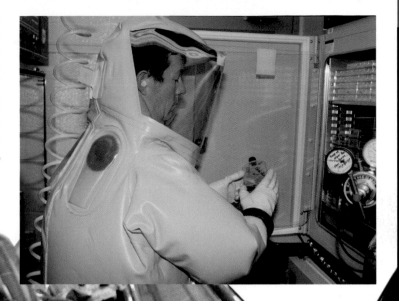

THE CLEANUP CREW ▼

When a dispatcher receives a call about a hazardous spill, a HAZMAT (hazardous materials) team is immediately dispatched to the scene to start the cleanup. These team members in Singapore are practicing what they would do if a chemical agent were released in a subway. Their gear is designed to keep toxins outside, away from the body. An air tank inside the suit provides clean air for breathing.

This mask filters hazardous chemicals out of the air.

Disposable hoods provide quick oxygen and protection in an emergency.

HEADPHONES

Is the thought of headphones music to your ears? It may be, quite literally! Headphones are small loudspeakers that convert electrical signals from a music player into sound waves that your ears can hear. Though most headphones work using the same principles, there are many different types on the market today. Some attach to a music player with a wire. Others are wireless, receiving infrared or radio signals that travel to the headphones from a transmitter attached to the music player. Some headphones cover the entire outer ear, while earbuds are small headphones that fit snugly in the ear. Noise-canceling headphones create sound waves that are the exact opposite of background noises. When the two sound waves meet, they cancel each other out.

5. The pulsing diaphragm creates sound waves that pass through a protective grill into the ear, where they are heard as sound.

4. The diaphragm is attached to the coil, and it moves when the coil moves.

3. The magnetic field of the coil interacts with the magnetic field of the magnet to create a force that moves the coil back and forth.

2. Electric currents travel through the coil, creating a magnetic field.

1. Electric signals from a music player travel through a wire to the headphone.

Magnet

Coiled wire

Diaphragm

◀ HOW HEADPHONES WORK

When you attach headphones to a music player, electric currents travel through a wire into a coil of wire wrapped around an iron bar. As electric currents move back and forth in the coil many times per second, the coil is alternately attracted to and repelled by a nearby magnet. This motion vibrates a layer of fabric called a *diaphragm*. The vibrating diaphragm pushes the sound waves into your ear canal.

did you
know?..................
DJS AND RADIO BROADCASTERS OFTEN
CALL HEADPHONES *CANS*.

▲ STEREOPHONIC SOUND

This colored X-ray shows a person listening to music through headphones. The red light represents the sound radiating from the headphones. Stereophonic sound occurs when headphones deliver different sounds to each ear. The brain processes the separate sounds into a complex soundscape. The next time you listen to music using headphones, notice how the sound jumps back and forth between your left and right ears.

HEARING LOSS

When a person no longer hears as well as he or she used to, that person has hearing loss. Temporary hearing loss may be caused by colds, allergies, infections, or earwax. Permanent hearing loss is most commonly caused by noise. When people listen to sounds that are too loud for too long, critical hair cells in the ear may become permanently damaged. Once damaged, these cells do not grow back. One study showed that 12.5 percent of people aged 6 to 19 suffer from noise-induced hearing loss. Hearing loss often begins when a person is a teenager, although it may not be noticed then. Age is the most common cause of hearing loss.

did you know? UNLIKE HUMANS, REPTILES AND BIRDS CAN REGROW DAMAGED HAIR CELLS IN THE EAR.

HOW DO WE HEAR? ▶

Hearing occurs when sound waves travel through the ear canal, vibrating the eardrum. These vibrations are transferred to three tiny bones in the middle ear—the hammer, anvil, and stirrup—which send the vibrations to the inner ear, or cochlea. The fluid in the cochlea moves, vibrating hair cells in the cochlea and creating an electrical signal. The signal travels along the auditory nerve to the brain, which translates the signal into sounds.

Muscle

Fat cells

Bone

Stirrup (stapes)

Anvil (incus)

Eardrum

Hammer (malleus)

Pinna

Ear canal

Ear lobe

HOW FRAGILE IS HEARING? ▼

Hair cells are fragile, and are easily damaged by loud sounds. Often hair cells that react to higher pitches are damaged first because these hairs vibrate more strongly, making them more likely to break. If your hair cells are destroyed completely, you will not be able to hear at all.

Hair cells

The hair cells closest to the stirrup detect higher-pitched sounds. The hair cells near the center of the cochlea detect lower-pitched sounds.

Cochlea

Eustachian tube

WHAT SOUNDS CAUSE HEARING LOSS? ▲

Sound is measured in units called *decibels*. A whisper measures about 25 decibels and a normal conversation measures around 60 decibels. Loud city traffic measures about 75 decibels. Each increase of 10 decibels means that the sound is 10 times more intense and sounds twice as loud to us. Prolonged exposure to any noise greater than 85 decibels can cause gradual hearing loss.

HOW LOUD IS TOO LOUD? ▶

Motorcycles can create sounds that measure from more than 100 decibels, even though by law they are limited to 80 decibels on the road. Scientists recommend no more than 15 minutes of exposure to sounds greater than 100 decibels. Other activities that put people at risk for hearing loss include snowmobiling, playing in a band, listening to fireworks, and cranking up the volume on MP3 players so high that other people can hear the sound coming out of them.

HOW TO PROTECT HEARING ▶

At 140 decibels, a jet engine is one of the loudest noises people can be exposed to. Some rock concerts, shotguns, and rocket launches also create sounds in this range. Sounds this loud can cause permanent hearing loss immediately. Workers exposed to loud noises, such as people working in manufacturing or construction, should wear ear protection and have regular hearing tests.

HEARTBEAT

Did you ever wonder what makes your heart beat? Like a pump in a machine, the heart squeezes and relaxes based on the careful timing of electrical signals. As the upper chambers of the heart—the atria—fill with blood, a mass of tissue called the *sinoatrial node* (sometimes called the "natural pacemaker") in the upper right part of the heart sends electrical signals to the heart muscle in the atria to tighten, or contract, and then relax. Once the atria contract, the electrical signal travels to a second node called the *atrioventricular node.* This tissue transmits the signal farther. The muscles of the heart's lower chambers—the ventricles—are then signaled to contract and then relax. This timed series of contracting and relaxing of heart muscle pumps blood through the circulatory system.

PACEMAKER ▶

If the heart's natural pacemaker, the sinoatrial node, is not working properly, the heart may beat too fast or too slow. This condition, called *arrhythmia,* can be treated with an electronic pacemaker. This X-ray shows a pacemaker that has been surgically implanted. The pacemaker can sense when the heart is beating irregularly. If that happens, the pacemaker generates an electrical signal that returns the heart to a healthy rhythm.

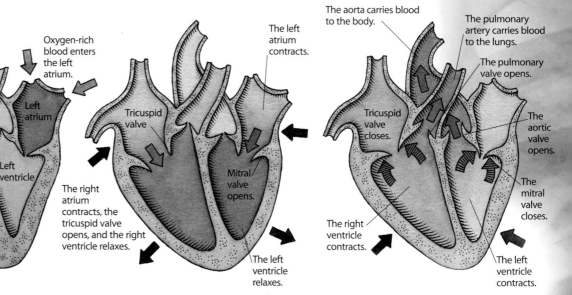

Oxygen-poor blood enters the right atrium.

Oxygen-rich blood enters the left atrium.

Right atrium

Left atrium

Right ventricle

Left ventricle

The right atrium contracts, the tricuspid valve opens, and the right ventricle relaxes.

Tricuspid valve

Mitral valve opens.

The left atrium contracts.

The left ventricle relaxes.

The aorta carries blood to the body.

The pulmonary artery carries blood to the lungs.

The pulmonary valve opens.

Tricuspid valve closes.

The aortic valve opens.

The mitral valve closes.

The right ventricle contracts.

The left ventricle contracts.

THE FLOW OF BLOOD ▲

When the atria relax, they fill with blood from the body. As they contract, the blood is pushed into the ventricles, which dilate, or get bigger. The ventricles then contract, pushing blood back to the body and lungs. Valves open and close to keep blood flowing in one direction. The cycle repeats again and again. The opening and closing of the valves also make the familiar, rhythmic sound of the heartbeat: lub-dub, lub-dub, lub-dub . . .

RECORDING THE HEARTBEAT ▶

A test called an *electrocardiogram,* or ECG, can tell if the heartbeat is normal. During an ECG, wires with sensors called *electrodes* are taped to the chest, arms, and legs. They sense the heart's electrical signals. These signals are recorded on graph paper. Doctors read the printout to see if the heartbeat is strong and regular.

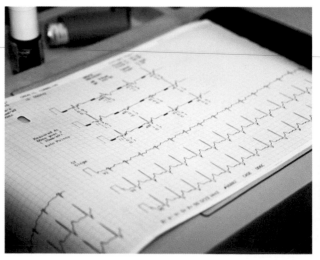

did you know?

AN ADULT HUMAN HEART PUMPS ABOUT 100,000 TIMES PER DAY. HEALTHY NEWBORNS CAN HAVE MORE THAN TWICE AS MANY HEARTBEATS IN A DAY.

A pacemaker is connected to the heart by one or more wires, depending on the type of arrhythmia a person has.
Heart
Wire to the atrium
Wire to the ventricle

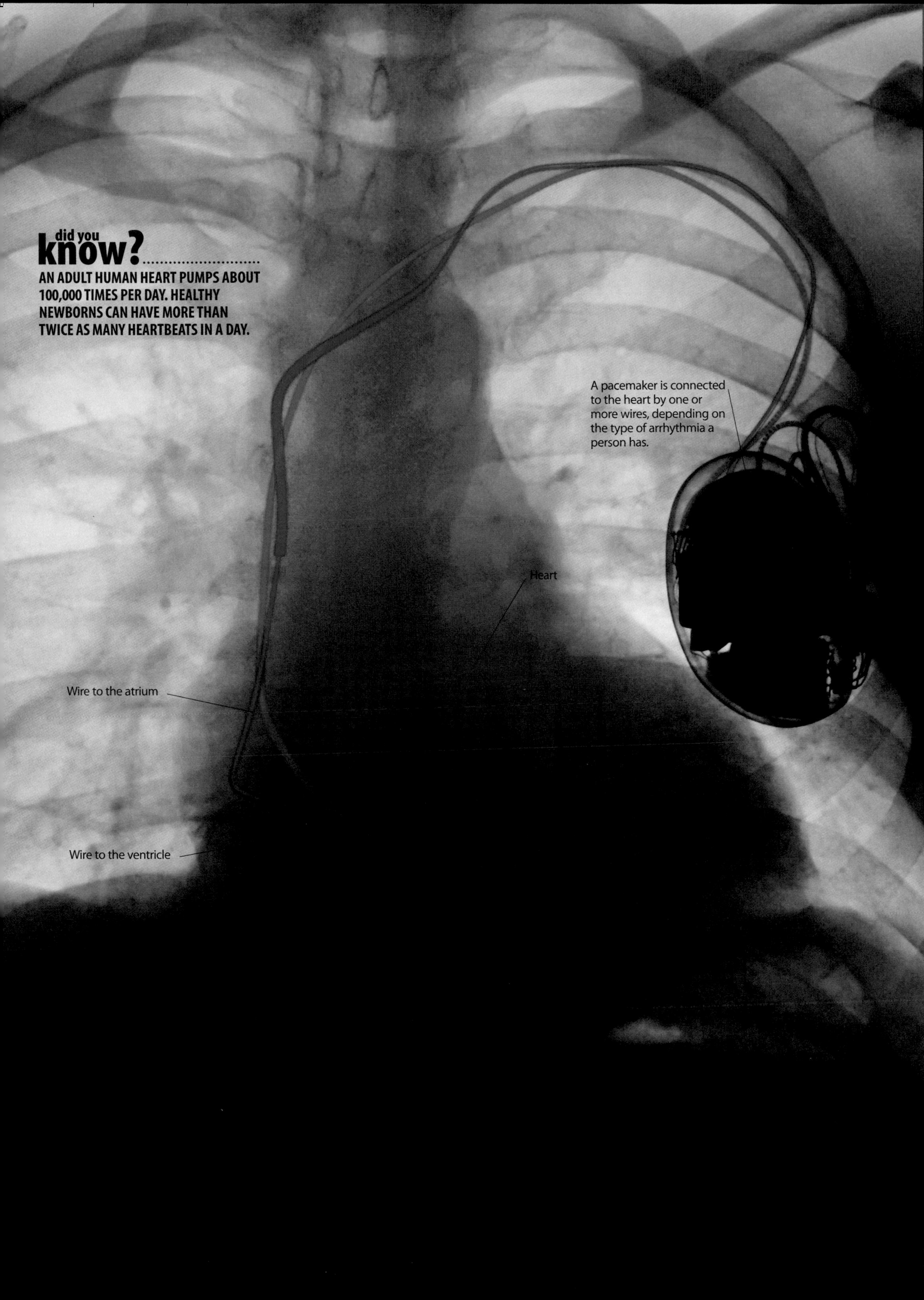

HIV / AIDS

More than 33 million people in the world today have the human immunodeficiency virus, or HIV. About 30 million of these people live in low- and middle-income countries. This virus infects a type of white blood cell of the immune system—the body system that fights disease and infection. Over time, a person with HIV can develop Acquired Immunodeficiency Syndrome, or AIDS. AIDS is a condition in which the body does not have enough disease-fighting cells. A person with AIDS can die from an unrelated disease—such as a flu—that a healthy person might easily fight off. Scientists think that HIV first infected humans who hunted chimpanzees that had the disease. The first known case of a human with HIV happened in 1959 in the Democratic Republic of Congo in Africa. HIV soon spread throughout the world and was first identified in the United States in 1981.

◄ FIGHTING THE DISEASE

When HIV first became known worldwide, people infected by the virus typically developed AIDS in about 10 years. Public efforts to help protect the rights of patients, to generate awareness, and to fund scientific research have greatly improved the outlook for HIV patients. Scientists have developed dozens of drugs that can keep the virus from taking over the body. There still is no cure for AIDS, but with such treatments, patients with HIV can live longer, more comfortable lives.

HOW THE VIRUS INFECTS CELLS ▼

Viruses are not living things. However, they are made up of molecules—proteins and genetic instructions—like those found in living things. A human cell infected by the HIV virus has copies of viral DNA in its own DNA. Those genetic instructions force the human host cell to make more viruses.

HIV virus (green) with membrane proteins that match up with host cell proteins

Host cell protein

HIV virus membrane combining with host cell membrane

Cell membrane

Virus's genetic instructions entering host cell

Virus's genetic instructions making virus DNA

Virus DNA combined with host cell DNA

Host cell DNA

◄ **EDUCATING YOUTH**

An important part of fighting the spread of HIV is educating young people on how the disease is spread. In 2006, the opening of this basketball court in Gaborone, Botswana, attracted many young people from the area. Here they attend classes on health, physical fitness, and how to protect themselves from risky behaviors that could lead to HIV infection. HIV can be spread through contact with an infected person's blood, semen, vaginal fluid, or breast milk. Thus, a baby can get HIV from its infected mother at birth or from drinking her milk. Children and adults can get HIV from sharing drug needles, touching a bleeding cut or wound, or having sexual contact with someone who has HIV. While some viruses can be found in saliva and tears, these fluids have never been known to cause HIV infection. A person's sweat does not contain the virus.

did you know?...................

THOUGH THERE ARE WELL OVER TWENTY DRUGS THAT CAN FIGHT HIV INFECTION, LESS THAN A THIRD OF THE PEOPLE WHO COULD BENEFIT HAVE ACCESS TO THESE DRUGS.

HOCKEY

When you play a game of ice hockey, whether you know it or not, you are demonstrating Newton's laws of motion—on skates! You chase after the puck and just when you think that you are going to get to it, an opposing player exerts a net force on you to change the direction of your motion. Once you manage to get to the puck, you apply a net force to it with your stick. It slides across the ice toward the net. You think that you are about to score a goal, but then the goalie's stick applies a net force back on the puck, sending it in the opposite direction. Just as Newton's first law predicts, the puck will continue to travel in that direction until a stick, a wall, or some other object changes its motion yet again. Newton's third law is involved in hockey, too. To skate, you have to push your skates into the ice so that the ice can push back on you, sending you forward.

▲ SMOOTH SKATING

Hockey players' skates are designed to slide across the ice with little friction to slow them down. Skaters use their legs to apply a force that pushes their skates against the ice. To stop, skaters turn their skate blades so that they are perpendicular to the direction they were headed, and dig the blades into the ice. In an indoor arena, a wall around the rink, called *the boards*, is sometimes the force that stops them.

Skaters wear helmets; padded pants; and shoulder, elbow, and shin pads to protect their bodies from the forces of impact.

Players use right- or left-handed sticks to control the puck. They apply force to the puck to make it move.

Gloves protect players' hands, help them maintain a grip on their hockey sticks, and keep their hands warm.

Long sleeves and stockings protect players' arms and legs.

◄ CHECKING

A body check is a deliberate collision to gain control of the puck. A skater uses his or her body to apply force to an opposing skater who has the puck. The force of the collision changes the direction and speed of the opposing player.

The goal is a net that catches the puck. The netting absorbs the force of the puck without breaking.

A goalie's larger helmet provides extra protection for the face and neck.

The ice for hockey games is about 3/4" (1.9 cm) thick, kept at 16°F (almost -9°C). The surface needs to be very smooth to avoid injuries to players.

A goal is made when the puck completely passes over the goal line.

Goalies wear extra padding and special leg pads to help stop the puck and to provide protection. They also use a special glove for catching pucks.

did you know? A PUCK IN PLAY HAS BEEN CLOCKED AT 105 MILES PER HOUR (ALMOST 169 KM/H).

HOLOGRAMS

The process of making and viewing a hologram is sometimes called "capturing" and "replaying" information, as if a hologram were music. Yet, like a photograph, a hologram is an image recorded on film or a plate—but in a very different way. A two-dimensional photograph, taken in normal white light, records the light reflected off an object. A hologram, taken using laser light, records the pattern formed by two intersecting light waves. To make a hologram, first a laser beam is split into two beams. One beam, called the *object beam*, strikes the object and reflects onto the film. The other beam, called the *reference beam*, strikes a mirror and then the film directly. At the film, the waves from the two beams meet and interact—creating what's called *interference*. The interference forms a pattern, which is recorded on the film's surface. When this interference pattern is illuminated, it reveals the three-dimensional hologram.

▼ TWO TYPES OF HOLOGRAMS

A reflection hologram, like this one of a great white shark, is visible in normal white light. A transmission hologram—typically a very detailed image—is visible when a laser shines through the film that captured it. Some of the laser light is diffracted—or redirected—by the interference pattern on the film. This light reconstructs the image that was captured on the holographic film.

did you know?...
IF YOU CUT OFF ONE CORNER OF A HOLOGRAM, YOU CAN SEE THE WHOLE IMAGE IN THAT PIECE, BECAUSE EVERY PART OF THE HOLOGRAM CONTAINS THE WHOLE IMAGE!

The shark's teeth appear sharp and three-dimensional because the hologram records interference of light reflecting off many sides of the object.

Each band of color
represents one
wavelength of light
emitted by the laser.

USING LASERS ►

Lasers are used to make holograms because
they produce light that is coherent, or
organized. Unlike white light, which
contains all the colors in the spectrum,
a laser produces a specific wavelength
of light. Different types of lasers are
used to produce light at different
wavelengths. The argon laser
shown here can produce blue
and green light wavelengths.

SECURITY HOLOGRAM ▼

Embossed, or raised, holograms
are commonly used on driver's
licenses, credit cards, paper
money, and product packaging.
Holograms make these items
hard to copy. The pattern of light
interference is recorded, and
then stamped onto clear plastic
or onto foil placed behind the
plastic. The foil reflects light with
the same pattern of interference
printed on the plastic or foil.

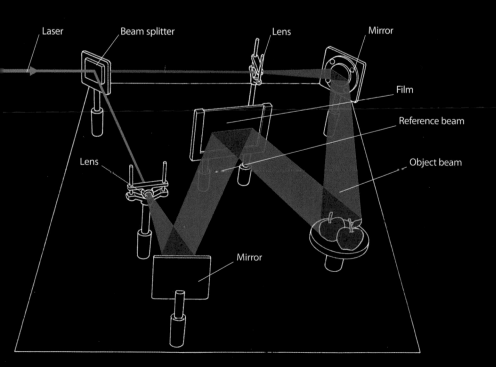

Laser   Beam splitter   Lens   Mirror

Film

Reference beam

Lens

Object beam

Mirror

HOODOOS

Hoodoos are tall, thin rock towers that project upward from flat plateaus. Hoodoos may be about the size of a person or as tall as a 15-story building. They form when rivers carve gullies in a flat plateau. Over time, these gullies expose walls of rock made of hard and soft rock layers. Water, ice, and wind erode the walls, and hoodoos are formed. Often the top layer of a hoodoo is a hard rock that forms a head shape that protects the softer rock below. Soft rock layers erode faster than hard rock layers, so the rock tower may be thin in some places and thick in others. But eventually, the softer rock erodes all the way through, and the tower falls to the ground.

did you know?..................

MANY HOODOOS ERODE FAST (BY GEOLOGICAL STANDARDS): ABOUT 2–4 FEET (ABOUT 1 M) EVERY 100 YEARS!

BRYCE CANYON, UTAH ▼

Millions of years ago, water covered much of western Utah. Layers of mud were compressed to form sedimentary rock. Then pressures within Earth pushed the layers of rock up to form a raised plateau. Rivers wore canyons in the plateau, until hoodoos formed. Today two types of erosion affect the hoodoos in Bryce Canyon. During the winter, melting snow runs into cracks in the rocks. At night, the water freezes and expands. This freezing and thawing causes rocks to break apart. Whenever it rains in Bryce Canyon, water combines with carbon dioxide in the atmosphere to form a weak acid. The acid dissolves the soft rock, but leaves the harder rock behind.

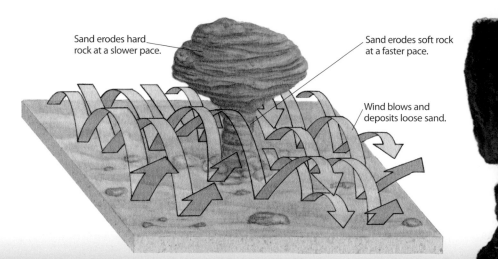

Sand erodes hard rock at a slower pace.

Sand erodes soft rock at a faster pace.

Wind blows and deposits loose sand.

The top hard layer, called a *capstone,* acts as an umbrella. It protects the softer layer below from the rain.

FORMATION ▲

Wind erosion shapes some hoodoos. When the wind blows loose sand particles against a rock tower, the friction erodes the soft rock layers the most. Hoodoos formed by the wind are round and smooth, while hoodoos formed by water and ice erosion are jagged and sharp.

THOR'S HAMMER ▶

Thor's Hammer is one of the most-photographed hoodoos in Bryce Canyon. Iron in the rock rusted to give the hoodoo a reddish color. Vertical cracks in the rock wear away, creating windows, or arches. Then the rock separates into towers to form new hoodoos.

HOOVER DAM

Engineers in the early 1900s saw a lot of potential energy in the Colorado River, where it flows through the Black Canyon on the border between Nevada and Arizona. They harnessed that energy by building Hoover Dam—a concrete wall that stopped the river's flow. The dam feeds river water into a hydroelectric power plant. This kind of power plant transforms the mechanical energy of flowing water into electrical energy. Water pulled down by gravity moves large, fanlike machines called *turbines*. Their spinning blades power generators, which produce electricity that people can use to power their homes. When demand for electricity is at its highest, 300,000 gallons (more than 1.1 million L) of water flow through the turbines every second.

Arizona

Four towers take in water above the dam and send it through pipes to the turbines of the power plant.

The road at the top of the dam is located 726 feet (about 221 m) above the rock at the base of the dam.

Hoover Dam is made of 4,360,000 cubic yards (more than 3,333,000 m^3) of concrete.

CREATING A NEW LAKE

Hoover Dam blocks the normal flow of the Colorado River, creating an artificial lake called Lake Mead. When the dam was finished in 1936, it had already started to flood the desert area above it, where the lake now lies. The small town of St. Thomas had to be abandoned in preparation for the dam. Some structures built by the people who lived there still remain under the lake's waters.

did you know?

THERE IS ENOUGH CONCRETE IN HOOVER DAM TO PAVE MORE THAN 6 SIDEWALKS THAT COULD SPAN THE DISTANCE FROM SAN FRANCISCO TO NEW YORK CITY.

◄ GENERATING POWER

The Hoover Dam power plant is located at the base of the dam, on the downstream side. The facility houses 17 turbines that can produce more than 2,000 megawatts of power—enough to power more than 200 million 100-watt light bulbs. The motion of the water spins the turbines, which causes a series of magnets to turn, creating a magnetic field. The rotating magnets spin past coils of copper wire, and this movement induces an electric current.

If the water level of the dam gets too high, water can flow on each side of the dam through overflow tunnels that empty downstream.

Nevada

HOVERCRAFT

Some boats reduce the friction between the water and the bottom of the boat by having a sleek, narrow hull that makes as little contact with the water as possible. A hovercraft, also called an *air-cushion vehicle (ACV)*, uses a different approach—it rides above the water! The boat's powerful engine pumps jets of air down and inward all around the edge of the craft. The air is trapped inside a flexible rubber skirt that surrounds the bottom of the boat. The skirt is designed so that its edge rests on the water, creating a seal and trapping the air. As more air squeezes in, the pressure of the gas molecules trapped between the water and the bottom of the boat increases, as it does inside a balloon, and the boat rises off the water. Propellers push the boat forward, and with no surface friction to slow it down, away it goes.

Propellers push air behind the craft to move it forward.

ZOOMING FROM DOVER TO CALAIS ▼

Hovercraft have been used as ferries in several countries. Between 1968 and 2000, the *Princess Margaret* was one of the largest ferries. In her heyday, she could carry 418 passengers and 60 cars across the English Channel in just over half an hour. The British ferries were retired because of the high cost of fuel and because people preferred to cross in the tunnel built under the channel. ACVs continue to be used for military operations, search and rescue, and transport to remote locations.

TO THE RESCUE ▶

A hovercraft can travel over land, ice, or water if the surface is smooth, or if the obstacles are smaller than the air space below the vehicle. One important use of hovercraft is as rescue craft in flooded or muddy areas where the water is too shallow for a boat and too muddy for a truck. The Canadian Coast Guard uses ACVs to break up river ice that would otherwise block the river's flow and cause flooding.

did you know?

THE FIRST FULL-SIZED TEST HOVERCRAFT, LAUNCHED IN 1959, CROSSED THE ENGLISH CHANNEL IN ABOUT 2 HOURS. LATER DESIGN IMPROVEMENTS REDUCED THE TIME TO 22 MINUTES.

Propellers

Air travels to huge fans.

The engine may direct some air out the back of the skirt to propel the boat forward.

Air is directed under the boat.

Fan

Skirt

MOVING AIR ▲

Propellers take in air and direct it to fans. The fans direct the air under the boat, and the air is held in by the skirt. A rudder at the back of the boat can be adjusted to steer the boat.

A longer skirt enables the craft to fly higher above the surface, making it more maneuverable in rough water.

HUBBLE SPACE TELESCOPE

When you gaze at the stars through a telescope on a cloudless night, you might think the view is crystal clear. But long ago, astronomers discovered that Earth's turbulent atmosphere distorts starlight. This meant that they could not capture razor-sharp images of stars, planets, and galaxies using ground-based telescopes. The Hubble Space Telescope changed all that. It creates clear images of objects in space because it is in orbit about 353 miles (almost 569 km) above Earth's surface. Like many other telescopes, Hubble uses a system of mirrors to gather, reflect, and focus light. However, in 1990, when Hubble was launched, scientists discovered that its mirrors could not focus correctly. In 1993, astronauts installed instruments to correct Hubble's "vision." Now Hubble delivers spectacular views of the universe.

The Hubble Space Telescope is 43.5 feet (about 13.3 m) long—a little bit longer than a school bus.

Flight operations instructs Hubble to close this door before astronauts service it. Light enters here when the door is open.

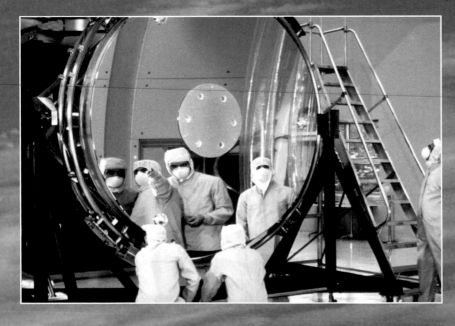

◀ EYE IN THE SKY

Hubble's concave, primary mirror is a glass disc 8 feet (2.4 m) in diameter. The disc is highly polished and thinly coated with aluminum. The primary mirror collects light and reflects it toward the convex, secondary mirror. The secondary mirror focuses and reflects the light back to the primary mirror. The light passes through a hole in the center of the primary mirror and forms an image. Scientific instruments record and read the image.

THE UNIVERSE—IN DETAIL ▶

Hubble's perch above the atmosphere allows it to create images that are 10 times clearer than those images produced by any ground-based telescopes. Even this early Hubble image, made before the telescope's "vision" was corrected, shows details of planets being formed in a region of the Orion Nebula. Since Hubble was first launched, it has helped scientists expand their knowledge of stars, planets, galaxies, and the history of the universe itself.

did you know? THE HUBBLE SPACE TELESCOPE IS NAMED FOR EDWIN P. HUBBLE, WHO DISCOVERED THAT THE UNIVERSE IS EXPANDING.

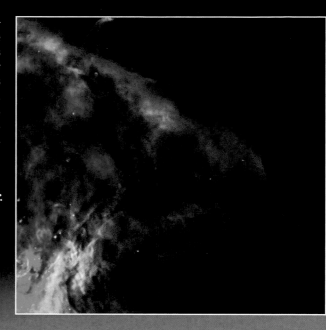

Solar panels convert sunlight into electricity. Hubble uses electricity to run all its systems and scientific instruments.

Control systems aim the telescope at targets and hold it steady as it records observations.

A reflective silver cover protects Hubble from extreme temperatures and small debris in the space environment.

Steerable antennas send data to communications satellites, which forward the information to computer systems on Earth.

◀ MORE THAN A TELESCOPE

In addition to gathering and focusing light, the Hubble Space Telescope serves two other purposes. It is a spacecraft and a station for scientific instruments. The ground-based flight operations team "flies" Hubble by transmitting instructions to its systems. The pointing control system (PCS) maneuvers Hubble into position and locks it on target—tricky business, since Hubble completes an orbit of Earth once every 97 minutes. A scientific instrument called *Wide Field Planetary Camera* has produced some of the most famous Hubble images. It works by detecting electromagnetic waves ranging from infrared waves to near-ultraviolet waves. Wide Field Camera 3 was installed during a 2002 servicing mission.

HUMAN GENOME

Scientists have put together a puzzle that has more than 3 billion pieces. The puzzle is called the *human genome*, a full set of all the genetic information in human DNA (deoxyribonucleic acid). Scientists already knew certain things about the puzzle when they began the Human Genome Project in 1989. They knew where to find DNA—in the nucleus of each human cell, on the structures called *chromosomes*. They knew what DNA looks like—a twisted ladder, with rungs made of four different chemicals, called *nitrogen bases*. They learned that DNA can be divided into 20,000 to 25,000 sections, each of which is called a *gene*. One gene might be made up of anywhere from thousands to millions of bases. To complete the puzzle, scientists had to learn the order, or sequence, of every one of the 3 billion bases. Different groups of scientists have worked on the puzzle, one finishing it in 2001 and another in 2003, and published the sequence of the basic human genome. The challenge now is to find out which human traits, structures, and diseases are influenced by which parts of our amazing genome.

READING FRAGMENTS OF DNA ▶

DNA sequencing that used to take years is now a much faster, automated process. Multiple fragments of DNA can be analyzed at one time. The process includes many steps between extracting the DNA from a cell and analyzing its sequence of bases. Liquid containing DNA is inserted into a thick gel, and in a process called *electrophoresis,* electricity is used to sort the fragments of DNA. The gel is then viewed on a lightbox that uses ultraviolet light (shown to the right). A computer analyzes the DNA sequence, identifying the order in which the four bases occur.

◀ SPELL CAT, TAG, ACT

The four nitrogen bases in DNA are adenine, thymine, guanine, and cytosine, which are referred to as A, T, G, and C. This computer printout shows the sequence in which they occur in a fragment of DNA. Every human gene has a particular sequence of bases. Some sequences tell a cell to make a particular type of protein. Others do not code for protein, and scientists are still analyzing their purpose. Scientists are working to understand how one DNA sequence translates into a protein found in a brain tumor, while another translates into a protein found in a healthy brain cell.

**did you
know?**..
THE LARGEST KNOWN HUMAN GENE HAS 2,400,000 BASES.
MISSING OR DUPLICATED BASES IN THIS GENE CAN CAUSE THE
MUSCLE-WEAKENING DISEASES CALLED *MUSCULAR DYSTROPHIES*.

HUMMINGBIRDS

It's hard not to be dazzled by hummingbirds. With their shining feathers of scarlet, ruby, and emerald, hummingbirds are the jewels of the sky. The tiny birds are also master aviators. They can fly up, down, forward, backward, and sideways, reaching speeds of up to 60 miles per hour (about 97 km/h). They can also hover, which they do with ease while feeding on flower nectar. There are approximately 320 species of hummingbird, but their ranges are restricted to North and South America. Hummingbirds are the smallest of all birds. The largest species—the giant hummingbird of South America—weighs about 0.7 ounce (about 20 g), and the bee hummingbird—the smallest bird in the world—is only 2.5 inches (63.5 mm) long and weighs barely 0.07 ounce (about 2 g). That's lighter than a penny!

COLORS GALORE ▶
South American countries have a wealth of hummingbirds. Just in Colombia, 133 colorful species can be found. Male hummingbirds are typically more brightly colored than the females, and more apt to be iridescent.

IRIDESCENT FEATHERS ▲
Hummingbird feathers, composed mainly of the protein keratin, are highly iridescent—they change color as the angle at which you view them shifts. Iridescence is produced by light passing through prismlike structures on the feathers' barbs. These structures create color by splitting light and scattering specific wavelengths back to the viewer.

The patch of bright, metallic feathers on a male's throat is called the *gorget*, which he flashes to attract mates.

Hummingbirds have 10 tail feathers, two fewer than most birds.

Hummingbirds have small feet that are not designed for walking. But their long claws and toes are perfect for perching.

Hummingbirds reach deep into flowers with their long beaks and lick up nectar with a long, grooved tongue.

HOVERING ▲

Hummingbirds get their name from the sound their wings make when they hover at flowers or feeders. Hovering is a unique form of flight, and it requires a lot of energy. When they hover, hummingbirds beat their wings between 10 and 80 times per second depending on the hummingbird's size—smaller hummingbirds beat their wings faster. Hummingbird wings are structurally different from those of other birds. Their wings connect to their shoulders with a ball-and-socket joint that lets them move their wings in nearly every direction. To hover, hummingbirds rotate their wings, instead of flapping them, in a figure-eight pattern.

Hummingbird mothers usually lay two eggs in their nest. The white eggs, about the size of jelly beans, are the smallest of all bird eggs.

Hummingbirds use sticky spider webs to "glue" the nest materials together.

did you know?...
HUMMINGBIRDS CAN REMEMBER THE LOCATION OF SPECIFIC FLOWERS THEY VISIT AND HOW LONG IT WILL TAKE FOR EACH FLOWER TO REFILL WITH NECTAR.

HOME SWEET NEST ▶

Hummingbird nests are remarkable structures. They are built by the female, and it can take her as many as 8 days to complete a nest. To make it extra comfortable for her offspring, she uses soft building materials such as lichen, moss, and cotton. To camouflage the nest from predators, the female will often plaster the sides with plant matter. Hummingbird nests are tiny, about the size of a walnut shell!

HYBRID VEHICLES

For the first hundred years in the history of automobiles, almost every car used the energy of gasoline to turn its wheels. In the past decade, though, more and more cars have begun to use an electric motor. Some electric cars run on batteries and plug in to recharge. Hybrid electric vehicles (HEVs) combine these old and the new technologies. An HEV motor burns gasoline or some other fuel, but the car also has an electric motor. Hybrid electric vehicles are twice as efficient as cars using only a gasoline engine. One way they save energy is by conserving the energy produced when the car comes to a stop. The electric motor operates as a generator and slows the car. This generator produces electrical energy, storing it in the battery to drive the car later. In a conventional car that uses gas, however, all of that energy to stop the car is transferred into heat with the friction of the brakes.

did you know?
THE FIRST HYBRID ELECTRIC VEHICLE WAS BUILT IN 1899, BUT IT COULD NOT COMPETE WITH THE POWER AND LOWER COST OF GASOLINE ENGINE TECHNOLOGY.

DOUBLE DRIVERS ▶
This view shows some of the parts inside a hybrid car. There are many different hybrid designs that put these parts in different places under the hood and under the body of the car. At least part of the time, HEVs use a fuel engine that is similar to a conventional gasoline engine. This engine is smaller, though, so it uses less fuel. When the car needs some extra energy, it comes from the electric motor. Some HEVs use only the electric motor when the car is driving slowly because gas engines are not very efficient at slow speeds. At stoplights, some hybrid vehicles shut the gas engine off completely. The electric motor starts right up when the stoplight turns green. In a city, this can save a lot of fuel!

DESIGNS FOR EFFICIENCY ▶
Hybrid vehicles are designed to save energy and make the best use of the fuel that they consume. The smooth curves of this car direct air around it reducing air resistance. Lightweight materials reduce the amount of energy needed to make the car move. Hybrids also are fitted with an electronic control system that ensures that the car always operates in the most fuel-efficient mode.

KEEPING TRACK ▶

Hybrid vehicles use computers to keep track of what is going on in the drive train, which consists of the parts of the car that transfer power from the engine to the wheels. The computer controls the gas engine and the electric motor by switching them on and off in a way that uses the combination most efficiently. The driver's display panel shows the speed and the amount of fuel left, and it keeps track of the battery charge and fuel efficiency. It also tells the driver which device is moving the car.

This gasoline engine is smaller than the ones used in fuel-only vehicles because it needs to provide only part of the power when demand is high.

The drive shaft helps transmit power to the wheels.

This system uses two electric motors. One is designed to work best at high speeds, the other at low speeds.

As in conventional cars, the transmission transfers the motion of the drive shaft into rotation of the wheel and axle.

A computer monitors the power demand and switches the motors and engine on and off.

Storage battery

When the car is stopping, the motors become generators that convert the car's motion to electrical energy to be stored in a battery.

DK EDUCATION

Design Miranda Brown and Ali Scrivens, The Book Makers
Managing Art Editor Richard Czapnik
Design Director Stuart Jackman
Publisher Sophie Mitchell

PEARSON

The people who made up the *DK Big Ideas of Science Reference Library* team—representing digital product development, editorial, editorial services, manufacturing, and production—are listed below.

Johanna Burke, Jessica Chase, Arthur Ciccone, Amanda Ferguson, Kathryn Fobert, Christian Henry, Sharon Inglis, Russ Lappa, Dotti Marshall, Robyn Matzke, Tim McDonald, Maria Milczarek, Célio Pedrosa, Stephanie Rogers, Logan Schmidt, Christine Whitney

CREDITS

The publisher would like to thank the following for their kind permission to reproduce their photographs:

Key: t-top; a-above; b-below/bottom; c-center; l-left; r-right

Cover and i) Getty Images: Discovery Channel Images/Jeff Foott (geyser); Shutterstock, Inc.: James Thew (lettering). **ii–iii)** Corbis: Bo Bridges/Corbis Sports. **iv–v)** Corbis: Paul Bowen/Science Faction. **vi)** Dorling Kindersley: Royal British Columbia Museum, Victoria, Canada. **vii)** Corbis: Jim Reed (b); NASA: ESA/The Hubble Heritage Team/STScI/AURA (tr). **viii)** Science Photo Library: Pasieka. **x–xi)** NASA. **4–5** Corbis: Chris Barth/Star Ledger. **7** Corbis: Diego Goldberg/Sygma (r). **8–9** Corbis: Lu Zhanhong/Xinhua Press. **9** NASA: Jacques Descloitres, MODIS Land Rapid Response Team at NASA GSFC (tla, tlb). **10–11** Corbis: Frans Lanting. **12–13** Corbis: Visuals Unlimited. **13** Dorling Kindersley: Natural History Museum, London (tr). **14–15** Corbis: Paul Bowen/Science Faction. **17** Dorling Kindersley: Dr. Brian Widdop, Medical Toxicology Unit Laboratory, New Cross Hospital (tr, cr, br). **18–19** Getty Images: AFP Photo/Max Hurdebourq. **19** Corbis: Gary Braasch (tl); NASA: Goddard Space Flight Center Scientific Visualization Studio (tr, cr). **20–21** Corbis: Schlegelmilch; Getty Images: Ferrari Press Office (tr, cr). **22** Dorling Kindersley: Natural History Museum, London (cl). **22–23** Dorling Kindersley: Natural History Museum, London. **23** Dorling Kindersley: Natural History Museum, London (tr). **27** Science Photo Library: David Parker (br). **28** Getty Images: AFP Photo/Yoshikazu Tsuno. **29** Corbis: Arctic-Images (tr); Tony Savino (b); Getty Images (cr). **32** Jongholee (cl). **33** Science Photo Library: Steve Gschmeissner (bc). **34** Science Photo Library: Simon Fraser/Newcastle-upon-Tyne (bl). **35** Corbis: IMANE/Image Point FR (tl); Science Photo Library: Dr. P. Marazzi (cl); Lea Paterson (r). **36** Corbis: Jerry McCrea/Star Ledger (cl). **36–37** Corbis: Jerry McCrea/Star Ledger. **37** Corbis: Jerry McCrea/Star Ledger (tr). **38** Dorling Kindersley: Natural History Museum, London (br). **38–39** Science Photo Library: Diccon Alexander. **39** Corbis: Maurice Nimmo/Frank Lane Picture Agency (br); Science Photo Library: Joel Aram (tr). **40** Corbis: Jim Sugar/Science Faction (l); Frank Lukasseck (r). **41** Corbis: Tom Stuart (r). **42** NOAA: Dann Blackwood/USGS (cr). **43** Corbis: Jeffrey L. Rottman. **44** Getty Images: Discovery Channel Images/Jeff Foott (cl). **44–45** Corbis: Glowimages. **46** Dorling Kindersley: Royal British Columbia Museum, Victoria, Canada (b). **47** Corbis: Paul Seheult/Eye Ubiquitous (t); Dorling Kindersley: Natural History Museum, London (b). **50–51** Corbis: Seth Resnick/Science Faction. **52** Corbis: DK Limited (b). **52–53** Corbis: Louie Psihoyos/Science Faction. **55** NHPA/Photoshot: Cede Prudente (tr). **56** Corbis: Paul Souders (l); Dorling Kindersley: PunchStock (br). **57** Corbis: Andrea Merola/EPA (r). **58** Corbis: Paul Souders (cl). **61** Corbis: Paul Souders (cr). **62** Corbis: Reuters (cl). **62–63** Corbis: Reuters. **63** Getty Images: AFP Photo/Jiji Press (cr). **64–65** Science Photo Library: Paul Zahl (c). **66** NASA (cl, c). **66–67** Corbis: Bo Bridges/Corbis Sports. **67** NASA (tr). **68** NASA: Jeff Schmaltz, MODIS Rapid Response Team at NASA GSFC (bl). **68–69** Corbis: Robert Estall. **69** Corbis: Michael S. Yamashita (tr). **72** Getty Images: Photodisc/Jeffrey Coolidge (bl). **72–73** Getty Images: AFP/Lim Wui Liang. **73** Getty Images: Greg Mathieson/Mai/Time & Life Pictures (tr). **74–75** Science Photo Library. **76–77** Photolibrary: Nucleus Inc./Phototake Science. **77** Corbis: Clouds Hill Imaging Ltd. (tl); Justin Guariglia (tr). **78** Science Photo Library: Antonia Reeve (br). **78–79** Science Photo Library: Gustoimages. **80** Corbis: Brooks Craft/Sygma (cl); Science Photo Library: Equinox Graphics (bl). **80–81** Getty Images: Per-Anders Pettersson. **82** Corbis: David Stoecklein (tr). **82–83** Corbis: JC Pinheiro/PressPhotoInt/Icon SMI. **83** Getty Images: Vladimir Rys/Bongarts (tl). **85** Corbis: Jonathan Blair (t); Science Photo Library: Andrew Syred (bl). **88–89** Corbis: George Steinmetz. **89** Corbis: Ian Austin/Aurora Photos (tl). **92** NASA (bl). **92–93** NASA: STScI. **93** NASA: C. R. O'Deil (tr). **94** Science Photo Library: James King Holmes (bl). **94–95** Corbis: Karen Kasmauski. **96** Corbis: George D. Lepp (cl). **96–97** Corbis: Mary Ann McDonald (tr). **97** Dorling Kindersley: Natural History Museum, London (br). **98–99** Corbis: Bruce Benedict/Transtock (background); Car Culture (car). **99** Corbis: Guy Spangenberg/Transtock (tr); Car Culture (c).

All other images © Dorling Kindersley
For further information see: www.dkimages.com